Ken has written a gift for every pressured, hurr[...] haunted person on the planet. So take a deep br[...] Slowly.

—**John Ortberg**, senior pasto[...]
author of *I'd Like You More If You Were More Like Me*

Loaded with practical insights and encouraging thoughts. Every reader will benefit from Ken's work.

—**Max Lucado**, pastor and bestselling author

This is only Ken's second book, but it feels like vintage material from an old soul. There's not a line here that doesn't brim with wisdom. Ken is a sensei master of the heart, and he shows us how to live well, deeply, and fully. This is *the* book for this generation.

—**Mark Buchanan**, author of *The Rest of God: Restoring Your Soul by Restoring Sabbath*

Like a great physician, Ken Shigematsu diagnoses our primary problem: striving to achieve in order to feel valued. He then offers soul solutions in the form of spiritual practices, such as Sabbath, service, and gratitude. He explains not merely the *how* of these practices, but also the *why*. This book will not only help your soul *survive*, it will allow it to *thrive*.

—**James Bryan Smith**, author of *The Good and Beautiful God*

At once immensely practical and deeply poetic, *Survival Guide for the Soul* gently instructs us in life-changing ways to stay intimately connected to God's love, grace, and peace. I will keep this beautiful and important book on my bedside table forever.

—**Suzy Welch**, *New York Times* bestselling author of *10-10-10: A Life Transforming Idea*; CNBC television correspondent

Ken has done it again: he has provided us with a gracious, compelling, and challenging call to live Christianly in the midst of the city—what it means to be women and men of Christian integrity in the midst of the temptations and expectations of urban living.

—**Gordon T. Smith**, president of Ambrose University; author of *Courage and Calling*

This book is a breath of fresh air to the soul! Those feeling burned out or bored with religion will find here a gentle invitation to return to spiritual practices as the simple, life-giving experience of being God's beloved. I don't just like this book—I need this book!

—**Michelle Sanchez**, executive minister of Make and Deepen Disciples, Evangelical Covenant Church

I cannot count the number of pages I have dog-eared—places where Jesus Christ broke through Ken's words to speak to and redirect and heal my soul. This book is a profound gift to the church and to the world and may well become a spiritual classic.

—**Darrell Johnson**, teaching fellow, Regent College; author of
Discipleship on the Edge: An Expository Journey through Revelation
and *The Beatitudes: Living in Sync with the Reign of God*

The power of the Christian message is not just its lofty and liberating ideas but also its practical and personal practices. In *Survival Guide for the Soul*, Ken Shigematsu acts as our masterful guide through the basic training of discipleship to Jesus. Thank you, Ken, for this gift to the body of Christ!

—**Bruxy Cavey**, teaching pastor at The Meeting House; author of
Reunion: The Good News of Jesus for Seekers, Saints, and Sinners

As a pastor of a large, diverse church and as a person who has deep knowledge of several cultures, Ken Shigematsu is keenly aware of the potentially toxic terrain in which we live. An astute spiritual pathfinder and trustworthy trail guide, he brings health and hope to the pilgrim seeking to follow Jesus.

—**Susan S. Phillips**, executive director and professor at New College Berkeley;
author of *The Cultivated Life: From Ceaseless Striving to Receiving Joy*

Full disclosure: I am mentioned a couple of times positively in this book and am grateful for the author's generous words. I recommend it with high enthusiasm, not only out of our long friendship but because it is full of scriptural substance and solid guidance. Take my word: through his wise insights Ken will be a good friend on your own journey.

—**Leighton Ford**, president, Leighton Ford
Ministries; author of *The Attentive Life*

A must-read for Christians at all stages of life. In this day and age when one's values are continually tested, we all need help in nurturing our very soul. Without one's soul, what are we other than dust in the wind?

—**Santa Ono**, president of the University of British Columbia (UBC)

I feel like this book was written for me. Much of my life, I've struggled with fear and insecurity and as a result, it's not that I think I have or am nothing, it's that I'm tempted to pursue everything—in hopes of achievement, worth, and purpose. What a beautiful book that reminds us how deeply God loves us and delights in us.

—**Eugene Cho**, senior pastor, Quest Church; author of *Overrated: Are We More
in Love with the Idea of Changing the World Than Actually Changing the World?*

This is not a book to read and ponder. This is a book to do. *Survival Guide for the Soul* offers a time-tested pathway for all those longing for depth, meaning, peace, and ultimately joy in a moment-by-moment friendship with God.

—**Tim Day**, director of City Movement and author of *God Enters Stage Left*

SURVIVAL
GUIDE
for the
SOUL

How to Flourish Spiritually
in a World that Pressures
Us to Achieve

KEN SHIGEMATSU

ZONDERVAN

Survival Guide for the Soul
Copyright © 2018 by Ken Shigematsu

The title is also available as a Zondervan ebook.

This title is also available as a Zondervan audiobook.

Requests for information should be addressed to:
Zondervan, *3900 Sparks Dr. SE, Grand Rapids, Michigan 49546*

Library of Congress Cataloging-in-Publication Data

Names: Shigematsu, Ken, 1966- author.
Title: Survival guide for the soul : how to flourish spiritually in a world that pressures
    us to achieve / Ken Shigematsu.
Description: Grand Rapids, Michigan : Zondervan, [2018]
Identifiers: LCCN 2018032173| ISBN 9780310535324 (pbk.) | ISBN 9780310535331
    (ebook)
Subjects: LCSH: Spiritual life--Christianity. | Spiritual formation. | Christian life.
Classification: LCC BV4501.3 .S54555 2018 | DDC 248.4--dc23 LC record available at
    https://lccn.loc.gov/2018032173

Cover design: Thinkpen Design, Greg Jackson
Cover photography: Isaak Dury, Noah Rosenfield / Unsplash
Interior design: Kait Lamphere

Printed in the United States of America

HB 04.27.2020

For Mom and Dad,

Your lives have shown me what matters most.

CONTENTS

FOREWORD

Ann Voskamp

The drowning keep to-do lists.
   Soul survivors keep rhythms.

This book is a survival guide providing rhythms for your soul—a survival guide for those who have been drowning in the pounding surf of life.

My daughter and I once sat at a table, a few blocks from the ocean, and enjoyed a long, lingering lunch with Ken Shigematsu. Ken is not a man tossed about by the waves. Every word he says or writes helps others survive the relentless tossing and churning. He knows that being deeply anchored in Christ cultivates rhythms, balancing the soul to ride out any storm.

I have witnessed firsthand how Ken tenderly guides, thoughtfully pastors, and sacrificially serves his community. His leadership is rare and his arms offer a wide, wise, and warm welcome, beckoning you to sit and be. When you're with Ken you know you are with someone who has spent intimate time with Jesus.

Reading Ken's book was like awakening to the music of *home*, like a hand reaching down to a drowning soul, ready to pull you out from the waves and carry you to shelter. The pages you are about to read may feel like a literal rescue. I read the book all the way through in one sitting, underlining and writing notes on page after page, rereading whole sections.

When I was done, I exhaled.

Every dawn is Day One. Today is made of fresh hope. These singularly sage and hopeful pages are a way for us to begin again and to keep beginning again and again, as we find and learn to *keep* the rhythms our weary souls yearn for.

Once, while I was reading to one of my daughters a story about a young woman who "put on her habit," our little girl reached up and patted my shoulder.

"What's a habit?" she asked.

I stopped for a moment, and then spoke slowly, carefully choosing my words. It was a "new dawn" moment for me, a fresh recognition of a familiar idea.

A habit is something that is worn.

A habit is what we wear. And a habit is *the way* we wear our days. If you consistently keep the same rhythms every day, you will keep your soul from growing threadbare. Consistently keep the same soul rhythms every day, and you grow deeper into Him, the One who will reweave your soul into glory.

Musicians play one right note after the next right note after the next right note. It's not an erratic splattering of sound or a fickle, helter-skelter banging of random notes. Music has order. It is composed. The notes played are intentional, considered, and deliberate.

Lives that have rhythm *sing*. They don't survive—*they thrive*. As I've read Ken's survival book for the soul, the refrain of these life-giving pages has kept me returning to my own rhythms.

I light a candle every day at the prayer table. And I write a bit in my journal, not mere words of mine, but Words of His copied out on the page. It's as if writing them with my own hand, shaping them with my own hand, can bring shape to my own life.

Only our own lack of love can keep us from His love letter.

Only being captivated by other words can keep us from His Word.

Keeping the rhythm of reading His Living Bread after every meal has been the singular most transformative habit of my life. And these patterns of our lives reveal the form of our souls. Take time to ask yourself, to reflect:

- Do we read more of His words than those on streams and screens?
- Do we intentionally practice habitual, unwavering gratitude or do the circumstances of our days control and form the tone of our souls?
- Do the rhythms of our sacred friendships and daily vocations consistently and congruently look cruciform?

While our habits clothe us—they also unclothe us. Our habits expose our wounds, our insecurities, our idols, our addictions, our chaos. But they also reveal our hopes, our dreams, our prayers, our steady souls. Our habits *are* us.

Habits matter because habits are the spine of our self-control. Habits are the small gears that leverage your life—and if you change your rhythms, you can change *anything* into a possibility. You change your life when you change how you meet Christ every day. Our rhythms become our everyday liturgy, the sacred cadence of the hours that reorient our tired souls.

Countless times I've watched my daughter sit before the white keys, her wrists arched, her fingers stretching into song. Each finger knows where to hit next. She hardly thinks about it. It's nearly automatic, an unconscious action. So go our daily songs and rhythms of the soul, the essence of our habits.

"Forty-five percent of what we do every day is habitual," say the researchers, "performed almost without thinking in the same location or at the same time each day, usually because of subtle cues." We play a note that becomes a subtle cue for another note to follow. We rise and pray. Or we check the internet. Or we go for a run. Day after day we practice and play our chosen series of notes, performing actions cued by other actions. As Aristotle wrote, "We are what we repeatedly do."

———————

Far too many of my days have felt a bit like—*drowning*. A flailing cacophony. It's hard to hold on to the rhythm when life keeps crashing in on every side. It's hard to survive in a world of relentless waves. And what Ken Shigematsu knows, what he shares in this survival guide, is this:

When it's hard to hold on, no one holds on to what is cool. *They hold on to Christ.*

They hold on to Him who is holy and healing.

When it's hard to hold on, we don't hold on to what's trendy. *We hold on to the True Vine.*

We don't hold on to the prevailing and the popular, we hold on to the Prince of Peace, the true Perfecter of our Faith. We only rise because of the gospel—the astonishing news that grace has grabbed the unworthy, and Christ cleans the unbearable, and God redeems the unlikely, and we live the unexpected.

I do not admire the term "progressive sanctification," for it is unwarranted by Scripture. *But it is certain that the Christian does grow in grace.* And though their conflict may be as severe in the last day of their life as in the first moment of conversion, yet he (she) does advance in grace—*and all their imperfections and conflicts within cannot prove that he (she) has not made progress.*

—*Charles Spurgeon*

Christianity isn't about growing "good"—it's about growing grace-filled and Christlike. Blessed assurance, Jesus assures us: *You don't have to pull yourself up by your bootstraps—you only have to pull close.*

And the lifeline of this guide by my friend Ken shows you exactly how to do just that, how to form spiritual habits that pull you close to Christ, wear Christ, savor Christ, commune with Christ, and survive, thrive and rise in Christ.

After our long lunch with Ken that day, as his words and wisdom were our feast, my daughter and I wandered down to the ocean. We walked the water's edge for hours. We watched the beating tides. And the ocean that day echoed what Ken and all soul survivors know:

The way to survive waves is
to keep the beat of your heart
in rhythm with the One
who walks on water.

Your guide awaits you.

Introduction

STRUGGLING WITH
MY STATUS

I recently mailed off a check to reserve a place at my thirty-year high school class reunion dinner. I'm looking forward to seeing old friends again, but part of me is anxious about going. I wonder if I will look older or younger than my classmates. Am I more or less successful? Are my spouse and family better looking? I know I shouldn't compare—but it's hard not to at a school reunion.

In our modern, industrialized world, we feel pressure to achieve in ways that people in previous eras did not experience. If you trace my family tree to the first half of the 1800s, you will see that every son took up the occupation of his father. If you explored your family history, you would likely see a similar pattern. Prior to the nineteenth century in most preindustrial societies, what you did was largely determined by the social circumstances into which you were born.

The landscape has changed. Now, we are able to climb professional and social ladders in ways that were impossible two centuries ago. From our childhood, we're told that if we work hard enough we can be anything we want to be. It's a powerful and exciting message. But what if you don't achieve your dream? What if you don't become rich, successful, and widely known? You may feel like you don't measure up or that you've missed out on life. Worse yet, you may think you are a failure. A person living in the Middle Ages, whose station in life was determined by their birth family, would not have struggled with this same sense of inadequacy and failure.

Twenty years ago, the self-help section of a bookstore was stocked with bestselling books that sold messages such as, "You can do it," "Anything is possible," or "Awaken the giant within you." These books sought to inspire us to *do more* with our lives, to achieve something spectacular. Today that message has shifted. Now bestselling self-help books are more likely to address how to cope with low self-esteem and shame, and overcome the feeling that we're not accomplishing enough with our life. As the Swiss-born philosopher Alain de Botton points out, "There's a real correlation between a society that tells people that they can do anything, and the existence of low self-esteem."[1]

I was raised in a global, urban culture where the pressure to achieve is especially strong. Born in Tokyo, Japan, one of the busiest, work-oriented cities in the world, I was two when our family moved to London, England. Then, when I was nearly eight, we moved to Vancouver, British Columbia, and lived there until I finished high school. After completing undergraduate studies in the Chicago area, I returned to Tokyo to work for Sony. While in Japan, I met Sakiko—the woman I fell in love with and eventually married.

On the night before our wedding in Tokyo, I went out to dinner with her dad, my future father-in-law. Although Sakiko had been born and raised in Japan, we were planning to move to Vancouver after our wedding. During the meal, my father-in-law asked me, "Would it be possible for Sakiko to return to Japan to visit our family from time to time?" As a very traditional Japanese man, he assumed that I might prevent his daughter from visiting her family if it inconvenienced me. "By all means," I replied, thinking that I would try to honor his request by returning for New Year's every year, because that season is very significant in Japanese society, much like the Christmas season in North America.

So we regularly return to Japan to visit her family. When I am back for New Year's, I am often wide awake at two in the morning because of the time difference. Sometimes I find myself asking "what if . . ." wondering what my life would have been like if my family had *not* moved away from Japan when I was a child. If I had grown up in Japanese society, there would have been enormous pressure on me to attend the right preschool, the right kindergarten, the right elementary school, the right junior high, and so on. Eventually, I would have felt the pressure to find a job at the right company and then the additional pressure to become a dutiful "salary man."

As I ponder what my life could have been, I breathe a sigh of relief: "Thank God I am not part of that relentless rat race!"

But if I am honest with myself, I know that I haven't quite escaped it.

I continue to feel that burden to achieve. I've been out of school for many years now, yet I have nightmares in which I'm a student, completely unprepared for a French or math exam. I still feel the pressure to perform during those crucial moments when others depend on me, as I felt when I played competitive basketball.

That pressure to achieve and succeed was there when I worked for Sony in Tokyo. And it has followed me in my work as a pastor. Even though some think of ministry as a less competitive, more "spiritual" vocation, I found that the transition from the business world to the church didn't free me from feeling that I needed to make something exceptional of my life and my ministry.

My good friend Jeff, who has keen powers of discernment, once told me, "For a long time, you have felt like you needed to be *the guy*. . . . When you were younger, you felt the need to be *the guy* on the football field; as a younger man, *the guy* in the business world; and now, *the guy* as the pastor."

His words moved me deeply. He was right. I *still* have that desire to accomplish something significant—to stand out in some way. That desire is strong in most of us.

Our desire to achieve may spring from a noble motivation: we want to make the world a "better place." Or it may be driven by fear, to avoid being labeled mediocre or that dreaded epithet: "loser."

Being completely absorbed in our work can make us feel fully alive, especially when we are doing what we were put on earth to do. But it can cause us to neglect our most important relationships. It can also lead us to neglect our soul—the part of us that communes with God and determines our true well-being and happiness.

As I look at my own life and talk with successful, driven people who have achieved impressive things, I find a common problem. Many of us understand *intellectually* that we are loved by God, but in our day-to-day experience we continue to base our value on our success, our outward appearance, and how others view us.

This is why I've written this book. It's an exploration of God's love. Knowing we are deeply loved by our Creator frees us to pursue a life of significant, enduring achievement—a life that is not driven by fear and anxiety but one that springs from a deep well of joy and gratitude for the love and grace God has shown us.

Twenty years ago, when I first came to pastor Tenth Church in Vancouver, I was intimidated. I felt nervous about the challenge of pastoring a historic church that had dwindled from more than one thousand to a little more than one hundred members. The congregation was elderly and primarily of European ancestry, and the church had cycled through twenty pastors (including associates) over the past twenty years.

On one of my first days at the church, the secretary told me, "Ken, I just want you to know that if this 'ship' sinks now, everyone will blame you since you were the last captain at the helm." She was trying to motivate me to work harder, but her words depressed me! During those days, I felt constantly anxious, trying to keep the ship of the church afloat. I wasn't doing this for the glory of God but to avoid humiliating failure. I didn't want to be seen as a loser. Today, that panicky anxiety is gone, in part because our church is no longer edging downriver toward a massive waterfall. But more than that, I now feel at peace because I know that whether I ultimately succeed or fail, God is with me. My peace has been nurtured by certain spiritual practices which remind me, regardless of my performance, that I am deeply loved by the one who matters most. God's love not only liberates me from unnecessary burdens, but it also energizes and inspires me for the work I do.

I wish I could say as I write this book that I've fully overcome my *drivenness to achieve*. But, as I look deep into my heart,

I know that even though I want to be faithful, I also want to be successful. Though I want to love God, I also want to be liked and respected by people. Though I want to be loyal to Jesus, I'm afraid of being average, mediocre, or ordinary. I'm anxious about whether I am accomplishing enough, whether *I am* enough. Because all of this is an ongoing struggle for me, this book is, first and foremost, a letter to myself.

In the chapters that follow, I will unpack the spiritual practices that help me experience God as someone who is alive and real in my everyday life. As I have grown more conscious of God's loving presence, I have found I have a more robust, healthy identity and an enlarged capacity to make a meaningful, lasting difference in the lives of other people. I'm finding there is a life of unexpected vibrancy and depth when I live with Christ at the center of my daily life.

This letter to myself is a survival guide of sorts. It's a guide to surviving the damaging effects of a driven life, a way of overcoming the need to succeed by living satisfied in the acceptance and love of God.

It's a survival guide for the soul.

PART 1

THE TWO "ADAMS" IN *Every Soul*

Chapter 1

THE DIVIDED SELF

For what I want, this I do not do; but what I hate,
this I do.

—THE APOSTLE PAUL, ROMANS 7:15[1]

A s 5 p.m. approaches, I feel a strong desire to remain at the office and answer one or two more emails, hoping to make a little more headway into my inbox. Yet I also feel the pull to go home and be with my family. Similarly, if we're married, we may value loyalty to our spouse but be tempted to fantasize about an affair with someone else. Or we might insist a healthy lifestyle is important but struggle with an irresistible urge to gorge at the dessert buffet.

We've heard people say, "Be true to yourself." But the truth is that we have *many* selves—not a single cohesive, unified self. Sometimes we feel as if there is a committee of voices within our heart, each vying for different, competing proposals. This isn't necessarily a bad thing. Scripture suggests that we are complex, multidimensional beings filled with a variety of motives and desires. Rabbi Joseph Soloveitchik, in his book *The Lonely Man of Faith*, points out that in the first pages of the Bible, the book of Genesis, we are given two different portrayals of Adam.

He contends that each of these "two Adams" correspond to a different side of our human nature. He simply refers to these as Adam I and Adam II.

Adam I and Adam II

According to Soloveitchik, Genesis 1 introduces us to "Adam I." This Adam is driven by God's command to "fill the earth and subdue it" (v. 28). He feels compelled to conquer, create, and control. In a modern context, this means that our Adam I wants to understand how nature works so we can conquer disease or create a thriving business or control our world. This Adam feels pressure to produce and be successful. Soloveitchik points out that this calling is good and necessary. We need a healthy amount of Adam I to get things done in the world.[2]

Soloveitchik continues in Genesis 2 by describing the persona of "Adam II." In contrast to Adam I's desire to conquer, create, and control, Adam II is led to a garden. He is called to serve it humbly (v. 15). A chapter later we read that Adam walks with God in the cool of the day (Genesis 3:8). The two Adams have different desires. While Adam I wants to produce goods, Adam II yearns for relationship. He longs to connect with his Maker and feels lonely until Eve appears. Adam II is not as interested in *how* nature works, but *why* nature is there in the first place. He seeks to find meaning in life.[3]

Soloveitchik recognizes that these two aspects of Adam reflect something true about every person: we each have this dual persona. Part of us strives for success (Adam I), while another part of us longs for connection with God and others

(Adam II). And these personas don't need to be opposed to one another. We all need a good dose of Adam I's drive and ambition to energize us for action—whether it's purging our garage, learning a new skill for our job, or seeking to make our world a place that reflects more of God's justice. But we also need to tend to Adam II's longing for relationship, spiritual connection, and meaning in life. A healthy person will find a balance between these two drives so they complement each other in a holistic, life-giving way.

I find both of these Adams alive within me. There is a Ken I, who loves to work and achieve, and a Ken II, who values relationships with others and treasures intimate moments with God. And I know that when one of these parts of my identity overshadows the other, it affects how I relate to my wife, my son, and the people around me. When these two Kens are not in balance, it shapes how I treat my body and engage my work.

What about you?

You have a (insert your name): _____ I and a _____ II. What do these parts of your heart look like? How does your drive to succeed affect your life and relationships? Does one of these two people dominate the other? Or do they work together, complementing each another?

I realize that it's awkward speaking of yourself with Roman numerals. So I've taken Soloveitchik's concept of a dual self and tried to further clarify *how* we are divided. One part of us *strives* to impact the world around us through our work and effort. And another part of us seeks *soulful* connection through relationships with people and by experiencing ultimate reality. In the chapters that follow I will refer to these two parts of our self as *Striving Adam* and *Soulful Adam*.

Whether you find yourself relating more to your Striving Adam or your Soulful Adam, the unrelenting push of Western society today is to feed and applaud our *Striving* Adam. Back when he first developed these concepts in 1965, Soloveitchik argued that Striving Adam was dominating Soulful Adam in our modern, Western society. Our ambition to conquer, create, and control usually wins out over our hunger to experience deep relationships with people and intimacy with our Creator.

Decades have passed since Soloveitchik first observed this, and now our world values even more the ambitions of Striving Adam. Our inborn drive for success continues to prevail over our heart's longing for meaningful connection. Today, people all around us are struggling to find wholeness and peace in their lives and relationships.

Pressure to Achieve in Education

A few years ago, when my son was still in preschool, his mother and I began to prepare admission applications for kindergarten. It seems a little extreme, I know. But Joey's preschool principal, whom we adore, had our best interests at heart in encouraging us to apply to a certain private school. She even suggested that we could improve his chances by taking a photograph of our son offering a homeless person a plate of turkey with gravy, cranberry sauce, and steaming mashed potatoes. She knew that I served as the pastor of a church with a feeding ministry for the homeless, and she thought the photo would strengthen Joey's application. We decided not to do that on principle—and, well, because I had a hard enough time persuading him to share his ice cream with me. We ended up sending him to our neighborhood public school, but when the public school teachers went on strike that fall, we thought maybe we *should* have taken the photo!

In the midst of the kindergarten application process, I was talking with an East Coast educator I know who shared with me that children today are experiencing more competition and pressure to achieve than ever before. Much of this burden, he said, comes from their own parents. Some parents begin registering their children for private elementary schools connected with elite high schools *on the day they're born.* They hire personal academic coaches for their fourth graders. They carefully track their child's involvement in sports, music, and volunteer activities for future university applications. "Kids have never been so messed up," my friend said to me. "And they're messed up largely because they feel so much pressure from their parents to succeed."

Edwin Friedman, a Jewish rabbi and highly respected family therapist, once said: "A child is healthy, in direct proportion to their having parents whose self-esteem is least dependent on their child's achievement."[4] In other words, Friedman believed that whenever a parent's self-esteem is dependent on their child's achievement, it leads to an unhealthy burden on the child.

> *Whenever a parent's self-esteem is dependent on their child's achievement, it leads to an unhealthy burden on the child.*

My niece Danielle lives south of San Francisco near Stanford University. Just before she began the eleventh grade she visited us, and she would often sleep past noon trying to catch up on sleep after endless nights staying up late to finish her vast homework load. Like many of her friends, Danielle felt pressure to get high marks so she could be among the top applicants for university admissions. The pressure was so intense that several high school students in her area committed suicide that year, jumping in front of trains. We're used to hearing stories about teenagers who hurt themselves or others because they are bullied or feel physically unattractive, but these are children who are killing themselves because they fear *failure!*

And the pressure grows even more intense when students graduate and enter the competitive workplace.

Pressure to Achieve at Work

Steve Jobs, who famously made many innovative contributions to our world through his Apple products, is a good example of what happens when a person's Striving Adam overshadows their Soulful Adam. Walter Isaacson, Jobs's authorized biographer, tells us that Jobs was so driven to create and succeed that he would forget his wedding anniversary, his wife's birthday, and the birthdays of his children.[5] While we can appreciate the amazing products his Striving Adam helped him make, it's clear that Jobs' drive to produce and create dominated the Soulful Adam within him.

When Apple was in the process of going public, Jobs refused to give any shares in the company to several of his closest founding partners. He saw the world through a competitive lens—and it was winner take all for him. In the 2015 film version of Steve Jobs' life, also based on the authorized biography, Steve Wozniak, the cofounder of Apple, tells Jobs: "Your products are better than you are, brother."

"That's the idea, brother," Jobs answers.

Wozniak doesn't let that pass. He fires back: "It's not binary. You can be decent *and* gifted at the same time."

That's the challenge, isn't it? Striving Adam's passion is to create great products. Soulful Adam's passion is to become, with God's help, a great person. And as Wozniak's character affirms, the two are not mutually exclusive. A person can be *both* productive *and* good. We need to find the balance between our Striving Adam's ambition and our Soulful Adam's longing.

One reason we often prioritize our Striving Adam is because we falsely believe that our achievements will help us overcome our sense of *not-enoughness* . . . filling the emptiness and making us happy. Psychologists tell us that our brains tend to mispredict what will actually bring us happiness. We assume that *if* we achieve certain things in our life, we will find happiness.

"I'll be happy *if* I get admitted into the right school."

"I'll be happy *if* I find the right partner."

"I'll be happy *if* I make vice president."

"I'll be happy *if* I have my dream house."

As Harvard psychologist Shawn Achor observes, this "if-then" perspective cannot be supported by science, because each time our brain experiences a "success," it moves the goal posts of what success looks like. If you got good grades, you now have to get *better* grades. If you have a good job, now you have to get a *better* job. If you hit your sales target, now you have to *raise* your sales target. If you buy a home, now you want to have a *larger* home.[6]

Each time we achieve something, a shot of dopamine gets released in our brain. We feel a rush, but it only lasts for a moment. After the initial flush of excitement, we begin looking on the horizon for another hill to climb, thinking that once we climb that hill, we will feel better about ourselves and happier. But when we ascend that hill, we hear the same recording again.

Christianity and Eastern religions both teach that the pleasure we get from money, possessions, and earned success can make us happy—but only at a very basic level. In order to experience the higher, more significant, and enduring forms of happiness we need something else. This happiness comes from *generativity*: bringing life and well-being to others and surrendering ourselves to an unconditional, infinite love.

This means that those who encounter God's love are uniquely positioned to live as whole, joyful human beings. As we embrace an unconditional, infinite love, we are freed from the vain pursuit of fulfillment through worldly success, and our contentment and happiness grows.

> *Enduring happiness comes from* **generativity:** *bringing life and well-being to others and surrendering ourselves to an unconditional, infinite love.*

As we are filled with this Spirit of love, we in turn impart life to others, and our sense of well-being deepens. Happiness is not the only goal of life, of course, but as we offer ourselves to God and find that we are being used as his instrument of life in the world, we experience a deeper, more enduring fulfillment as well.

When we live from this place of joy, rather than sacrificing our accomplishments, we often become even more productive.[7]

During my early years at Tenth Church, I felt desperate to see the church experience a turnaround. I was clocking seventy-hour work weeks, but my efforts weren't bearing fruit. We would experience a little growth, but just around the corner face discouraging decline. When I got married, I cut back my work week and something surprising happened. Even though I was working fewer hours, my ministry became more fruitful. The church grew healthier. Fast forward several years—I became a parent, and I reduced my work week further still. Again, I found that while my family life improved, the church thrived as well.

What made the difference? As I scaled back my work hours, I began to embrace certain spiritual practices—including meditative prayer and specific gratitude exercises—which deepened my sense of connection to God and enabled me to be more present to my family and those around me. Because of this, my work began to flourish. I still feel the pull at the end of the workday to stay in the office a little longer and answer a few more emails. But I've learned over time that a small sacrifice in one area of my life and a corresponding investment in another area can lead to a fruitful balance where *striving* Ken and *soulful* Ken work together in harmony.

As we move ahead, I want to introduce you to several people from history, including Augustine and Dorothy Day, as well as several contemporary figures who have cultivated a rich, joyful inner life with God while also engaging in meaningful, significant work in the world. They all faced real pressure to achieve. But their lives show us that it's possible, even in a divided world, to live with a whole and beautiful soul.

Questions *for* Reflection and Discussion

———◇———

1. Are you more naturally inclined toward Striving Adam or Soulful Adam? How is this evident in your life?
2. Do you feel compelled to validate your existence through your education, work, a relationship, your appearance, or in some other way?
3. Do you know anyone who integrates well both the Striving Adam and Soulful Adam parts of themselves? If so, what is that person like?
4. What is the difference between achievement and fruitfulness?
5. How can feeling content lead to greater fruitfulness?

Prayer

Lord, teach me your ways that I may live by your truth. Give me an undivided heart that I might honor you.

                                                    –SEE PSALM 86:11

Chapter 2

THE WHOLE SELF

The greatest temptations are not money, sex, and power, but self-rejection—because self-rejection contradicts the sacred voice that calls us the beloved.[1]
–HENRI NOUWEN

I n my early twenties, I visited the Hiroshima Peace Memorial Museum in Japan. There I saw firsthand the graphic devastation caused by the atomic bomb, which killed more than a hundred thousand people and destroyed the city in a matter of several minutes. The experience was deeply disturbing for me, personally, as my father had grown up just south of Hiroshima. He had passed through the decimated city a mere six days after the destructive blast.

In the museum, wax figures depict people who were exposed to the atomic bomb, their limbs folded and twisted like melted wax. Those who survived the blast were exposed to high doses of radiation causing them to suffer leukemia and cataracts as well as cancers of the thyroid, lung, and breast. Pregnant women gave birth to children with smaller brains and mental retardation.

Genesis 3 teaches that the human race has been similarly affected by our sin. Each one of us has been compromised by the radioactive devastation of sin, which causes defects in our desires and behaviors. Deceived by the seductive promise of becoming gods themselves, Adam and Eve turned away from God. Their alienation from the Creator—the source of all that is good, true, and beautiful—left them ashamed in each other's presence and afraid of their Maker. They covered their naked bodies with fig leaves and hid in the bushes.

Like Adam and Eve, we are lured into believing that we can take control of our lives. We foolishly believe the lie that we can become like God through independence from him. As we turn away from our Creator, our hearts experience distorted desires for pleasure, power, and privilege—which in turn breed shame, fear, and alienation from God, our true selves, and one another. Our disfigured desires cause us to feel dis-ease before God, leading to further distortions of desire that draw us farther away from true ease and happiness.

When Jesus Christ gave up his privilege as the Son of God by willingly laying down his life on the cross, his love brought healing to the radioactive effects of sin. His work on the cross reconciles us with God and restores our good, true, and beautiful desires so that we might share the mind and heart of Christ. This means that the most powerful way to cultivate a healthy Soulful Adam—enlivened by God's Spirit—is not by commanding ourselves like a drill sergeant to live the "right" way, but through a living relationship with Jesus, the true lover of our soul. Like the oboe player, who plays a clear, penetrating A for an orchestra and enables the other players to adjust their

Like the oboe player, who plays a clear, penetrating A for an orchestra, the transformative love of Jesus Christ tunes the desires of our souls.

instruments to a unified pitch, the transformative love of Jesus Christ tunes the desires of our souls.

The life of Augustine, who emerged as one of the greatest church fathers and theologians of the church, gives us an example of what a life attuned to the love of Christ looks like.

Reordered Affections

Augustine was born in 354 AD in the North African city of Thagaste (modern-day Souk Ahras in eastern Algeria). His father, Patricius, was a small landowner of modest means, but he and Augustine's mother, Monica, had great ambitions for their bright and talented son. Although he was a bit mischievous as an adolescent, Augustine was intellectually brilliant, and he attracted the attention of a wealthy patron named Romanianus, who agreed to sponsor Augustine's education. When he was seventeen, Augustine went to Carthage to study, excelling in classics and rhetoric. Like many young people today, he was driven to succeed. Longing for the praise of others, he "panted after honors"[2] and "wanted to live in the mouths of people forever."[3]

After completing his studies, Augustine became a teacher of rhetoric in Carthage and then a professor of literature in Milan. Eventually he won the great honor of speaking on behalf of the emperor at the Imperial Court in Rome—a supreme signature of success.[4] Yet his drive to succeed was accompanied by another pattern of equally insatiable desires. His sexual appetite resulted in a child with his mistress, yet at his mother's urging, he dropped that relationship in favor of a marriage that would elevate his social standing. Then, while he waited two years for the girl to reach a suitable age for marriage, he secured a concubine to satisfy his sexual urges. By cultivating his talents and selectively choosing his associates, Augustine sought to be the master of his fate and the captain of his soul. By all accounts, he was living the dream. His star was rapidly rising, his fame was growing, and he had an active sex life.

Yet, by his own admission, none of these things brought him lasting peace or happiness.

Paradoxically, as Augustine became more successful, he grew ever more dissatisfied. As he later wrote in his *Confessions*: "Our heart is restless until it rests in you."[5] Awakening to the impulses of Soulful Adam, he considered the possibility of withdrawing from the world for a life of contemplation, telling his friends that worldly ambition was a source of foolish suffering. Ambition, he told them, obliged him to "drag the burden of my unhappiness with me."[6] Although Augustine sensed God wooing him, he resisted. He knew that committing his soul to God would deprive him of the worldly pleasures he enjoyed. On the one hand, he longed for Christ to make him the virtuous person he wanted to be, yet there was something else holding him back. He felt he wasn't ready for such a commitment. "Make me pure," he prayed, "but not yet."[7]

One day, when he was about thirty years old, Augustine found himself in a small garden in Milan. His heart was in a tumult, and he heard a child's voice speaking. "Take and read. Take and read it." Sensing that the voice was speaking to him, he grabbed a Bible, opened it, and read the first passage he saw: "But put ye on the Lord Jesus Christ, and make not provision for the flesh, to fulfill the lusts thereof." Light flooded his soul. The shadows were swept away. He felt a new desire to renounce worldly, temporal pleasures and to pursue a life for Christ. He would later describe how, as he was moving toward the pinnacle of success, he was "saved from worldly ambition."[8]

Wanting to make a clean break from his lifestyle of ladder-climbing and sexual indulgence, he returned to the city of his birth. In Thagaste, Augustine established a small monastic community of faith to foster contemplation and the study of Scripture. As he daily encountered the living God and developed a growing life of prayer, Augustine's desires were reordered: "What I could have been [and wanted to be], I wished not to be."[9]

Augustine assumed that he would spend the rest of his life in this obscure monastic setting, but providence guided him elsewhere. On a trip to the coastal city of Hippo to counsel someone, the local congregation seized him and brought him before the bishop, asking that he be ordained as their pastor.[10]

And so began a ministry of pastoring and writing that would alter the history of the church.

As a young man, Augustine had wanted to live a richly sensual life. He had nurtured a desire to be famous. And while his desires were transformed by his encounter with Christ in the garden, they were also mysteriously fulfilled in unanticipated ways. Though Augustine committed himself to a life of celibacy, he would find deep fulfillment feeding on Christ through the sacramental bread and wine. And while he no longer pursued fame, he would eventually become one of the best known Church Fathers, a monumental figure of history.

From Ambition to Integrity

The story of Augustine is helpful because it illustrates how God works in our lives today. As we are drawn close to God, our desires are also redeemed and enlarged. And as Augustine discovered in the fourth century, those desires are often fulfilled in unexpected ways. Surrendering our lives to Christ not only radically recalibrates our desires, it also brings us into a more—not less—fulfilled life. When we look back, we find that God's ways are far better than our own (Isaiah 55:9).

I have seen this dynamic at work in the life of my mother, who grew up in a Japan that had been impoverished by World War II. By working hard, she excelled at a Tokyo high school, and then, at a time when very few Japanese students were able to study abroad, she earned a bachelor's degree from the University of California at Berkeley. She went on to complete a master's degree at Columbia University in New York. Eventually, she had five children and, like countless mothers across the ages, began projecting her Striving Adam's ambition for success onto her children. Mom made it clear that her great hope was that we would all attend graduate school. That was her idea of a successful life.

My mom worried about me while I was growing up because I had no interest in studying. In elementary school, I hated reading, but I loved playing street hockey. So my mother made me a deal: I could play hockey in the cul-de-sac in front of our home if—and only if—I would write a one-page book report. So I would sit at the desk in my room with tears streaming down my face, staring longingly through the window as the neighborhood kids played hockey. Over the years, I wrote many of these one-page reports, and they were all strangely similar: the title of the book, a comma, and my stock review sentence—"This was a pretty good book."

How do you make that one sentence into a full-page book report?

You use a big fat Sharpie!

Even though I desperately wanted to play ice hockey, the equipment was expensive and our family didn't have much money. The practices were also dreadfully early. Again, my mom bribed me with a promise. "If you get straight A's in school, you can play." At the time, I was a straight D student. But because I loved hockey, I eventually got those straight A's. Of course, as soon as I started playing hockey, those A's reverted back to D's.

When I was a teenager, my mother recommitted her life to Christ, and something changed in our home. The passions and desires of Soulful Adam began to lay claim to the landscape of her heart. Her values shifted, and she no longer pressured us children to perform academically. As she grew to understand God's gracious love for her, she was freed from the need to impress others. My mother became more confident in God's provision for her, and over time her concerns shifted to something far greater for her children than good grades and getting into the right school. She longed that we would follow the way of Christ and become people who faithfully reflect his character.

In high school I began applying to several universities, and I clearly remember what my mother said to me: "You should not choose a school based on its prestige or the income-earning potential of its graduates. You should choose a school that will help you fulfill God's calling on your life." A couple of years later, when my younger sister was in junior high school, my mom said something similar to her: "Intelligence is important, but becoming a person of kindness is even more important." After meeting Jesus Christ and giving herself to him, a robust Soulful Adam flourished in my mother's heart. As she was filled with God's love, her vision for others became grander, and she grew less anxious and more joyfully content.

Ironically, all five of her children would go on to earn graduate degrees. But the earlier educational ambitions she had for our lives didn't hold significance for her anymore. Her ambitions had been made new by God. As her desires were crucified, resurrected, and fulfilled in Christ, she gained something far greater than the fleeting satisfaction of worldly success: the depth and enduring happiness that comes through a rich relationship with God.

I want to be clear. The desire to achieve in academics, music, sports, ministry, or our careers is not intrinsically wrong. These desires can be noble, even birthed by God. But when Christ is at the center of our lives, our primary ambition becomes incomparably greater. We long to know Christ deeply and honor his call to transform our broken world so that it reflects the justice and beauty of God's kingdom.

From Breadth to Depth

As our ambition is redeemed, we are freed from the need to succeed in a worldly sense, and empowered instead to live with depth and integrity. Even if we achieve success by the world's standards, we won't be driven by a compulsive need. Having a healthy Soulful Adam means that we don't need to be successful, rich, or widely known in order to win the respect and approval of others. This frees us to pursue the will of God for our lives.

My mentor and close friend, Leighton Ford, embodies this joyful freedom in his vocation. When he was only fourteen years old, Leighton began preaching with Youth for Christ, a ministry to high school students. Because Leighton was unusually tall and mature for his age, his ministry supervisor thought he was eighteen years old and entrusted him with a lot of responsibility in the ministry! Leighton was ambitious for God, and with an earnest Striving Adam, he yearned to have a significant impact.

After graduating from Wheaton College, he wed Billy Graham's sister, Jeanie, and became part of the "royal family" of the Christian world. A rising star, Leighton began preaching in large football stadiums around the world. The Religious Heritage of America named him Clergyman of the Year, and *Time* magazine identified him as the person most qualified to succeed his famous brother-in-law, Billy Graham.

Leighton's son, Sandy, had become an accomplished track and field runner. Unexpectedly, he was diagnosed with a rare heart disease that caused arrhythmia (irregular heartbeats). After an operation to address his condition, Sandy seemed fine. But then, while running with a college roommate shortly after his twenty-first birthday, the arrhythmia struck again. A few days later, he died on the operating table.

Sandy had been a student leader at his university. He was in love with a young woman, and like his father, he aspired to become a minister of the gospel.

A few days after Sandy's funeral, Leighton went to Sandy's room near the university to gather his son's belongings. He came across a journal by Sandy's bed and it opened to a passage his son had written while in France on a mission trip the summer before:

> I still have dreams of what I would like to do and what life
> should be. But I am beginning to realize that life to me is
> really short.

As he looked over to Sandy's desk, Leighton found an unfinished poem. It was titled "To Dad, for his fiftieth birthday." The words of the poem remain etched on Leighton's heart to this day:

> What a golden honor it would be to don your mantle,
>   to inherit twice times your spirit.
> For then you would be me and I would continue to
>   be you.

Leighton wept. He thought of the promise of this beautiful life, a promise that would no longer be fulfilled, a mantle that would never fall on his son's shoulders.

In the midst of his searing loss and pain, Leighton felt God drawing close to him. He sensed the Holy Spirit calling him to begin a new ministry, one that would mean stepping out of the limelight. He felt led to invest himself into a small group of younger men and women to help them "run their race" for God through one-on-one spiritual mentoring. Leighton's suffering and his experience of God's love clarified what was most important. His pain, paradoxically, freed him from the need to pursue the path of conventional success.

Even though Leighton's new ministry was humble and obscure compared with his rock-star stadium evangelist status with the Billy Graham team, his original vision to make a difference in people's lives has been fulfilled in a beautiful and unexpected way. Over the decades Leighton has continued to walk with a small number of people in a deeper way as "an artist of the soul and a friend on the journey." And over time, the ripple effect of one dedicated life has been felt around the world, across generations, and into eternity. Leighton's young mentees are empowered "to lead more like Jesus and more to Jesus."

Through an unassuming ministry of spiritual direction, Leighton, now in his eighties, has been blessed with many sons and daughters. He is no longer an "A-list Christian celebrity," as he once was in his younger years. But his influence is deep and wide. And he is now at home in his own skin, truly content with his life and calling. He models the marriage of a healthy striving ambition and a soulful investment in personal relationships of love and depth. As Sandy's poem foretold, the mantle of Leighton's ministry has fallen—not on Sandy, but on his many spiritual sons and daughters.

From Fear to Love

People such as Leighton Ford, who can freely choose to walk away from a successful or significant career, do not live in fear of failure. They live out of a strong sense of self-identity rooted in a deep knowledge of God's love and acceptance.

If you are anything like me, you long for this kind of contentment and security in your own life. We all struggle with the fear that our lives don't measure up. We all long to be seen as significant in the eyes of someone important, perhaps a parent, a boss, a teacher, or a friend. Sometimes the goal is to meet our own impossibly high self-expectations. But regardless of the standard we are seeking to meet, our fundamental problem is not having too strong a sense of our self but too weak a sense of self. The path to true satisfaction is not the loss of our Striving Adam but the marriage of our ambition with the soulful satisfaction of being loved by God.

I often feel a gnawing deficiency in myself when I am introduced to an attractive or successful person at a party, or when I hear about a colleague who is advancing professionally more quickly than I am.

> *Our fundamental problem is not having too strong a sense of our self but too weak a sense of self.*

Even people who seem self-assured can feel inadequate on the inside. They may project a false confidence to cover up a sense of their inadequacy.

I know that I'm feeling this way when I catch myself bragging, name dropping, or exaggerating my achievements. These are sure indicators that I am afraid I won't be accepted.

Part of what fuels our drive to succeed is our need for the acceptance and respect of others. But the antidote to that need isn't merely a little more acceptance and respect. It's a *deeper* experience of acceptance and love. When we truly know that we are accepted and loved by our Maker, we won't be so desperate to fill what is lacking with the recognition we receive from others. Oddly enough, we become less concerned about what others think of us.

Braden is a five-year-old soccer player who showed up on the first day of practice for our local community league. At the practice, he was bullied by some older kids, and when Braden's father saw the other boys taunting and teasing his son, he quickly turned into a protective father bear.

But before his father could intervene on his behalf, Braden responded to the kids.

Stretching himself to his full height, Braden put his hands on his hips and stuck out his chest. "I am not a stupid little jerk," he told the bullies. "My daddy says I'm a soccer player."

Braden's knowledge of what his father thought about him had greater power than the strength of the bullies. That knowledge of his father's love and approval protected his identity, shielding him from the insults of his peers and giving him strength to face them.

When we realize, through the help of the Holy Spirit, how much God our Father loves us, we will become less concerned about what others think.

From Competition to Calling

God transforms our experiences of rejection by healing us through his perfect love, which shields us from fear. The apostle John wrote that "perfect love drives out fear" (1 John 4:18). This means that as God nurtures a healthy, robust sense of confidence within us, we will be freed from the need to compete and compare ourselves with others.

Stephen, a young professor at one of the world's greatest universities, was being considered for tenure because of the enormous contributions he had made to his institution. It was unusual for someone his age to be considered as the school almost never granted tenure to young faculty members.

The academic dean selected Stephen and a female colleague as nominees for a very prestigious academic fellowship, the prize for which was a hefty financial gift as well as access to an elite academic circle. Knowing that his institution could only put forward one nominee for the fellowship, Stephen approached his female colleague and suggested that they help each other by reading each other's applications and trying to improve them. Weeks later, once the applications were submitted and the review process completed, the dean invited Stephen into his office and informed him that he had been the one chosen. His name would be submitted for the competition.

What Stephen did next seems unbelievable to most people.

Thanking the dean, he told him that he didn't think he deserved it. "I worked on my colleague's application," he said. "Here's what you're missing. Here's what's brilliant about what she's doing." His words had the desired effect. Stephen changed the dean's mind, and instead of his nomination being submitted, the dean put his colleague forward as the nominee instead.

Now why would anyone do this? This wasn't false humility. Stephen had written brilliant papers that had helped net fifteen million dollars in grant money for his school. Stephen was ambitious—he had a robust Striving Adam. But he was honestly convinced that his colleague's application was superior. And as a committed follower of Jesus Christ, Stephen knew that his identity wasn't dependent on winning a prize. Would he have enjoyed winning? Of course! But Stephen knew that he was deeply loved by God. His inner nakedness had been covered by grace. So he didn't need to be successful in a worldly sense. He was free. Free to pursue something far grander and more joy evoking: God's will for his life. Because of his close relationship with God, Stephen's ambition was at the service of his calling, not in service to himself. And because his desires were rightly ordered, he was deeply satisfied and fulfilled.

From Drivenness to Grace

If we are driven to accomplish great things *in order to* be loved, we are slaves to success. We will climb the ladder of success out of a sense of deprivation, and even if we reach the top we will still feel unsatisfied and empty. But there is another way. If, like Augustine, my mother, Leighton, and Stephen, we seek to make significant contributions to the world *because* we are loved, we are now living as children of grace. We will see everything we have as gift. We will be motivated to do our best work out of deep gratitude.

When my mother-in-law was pregnant with Sakiko, who is now my wife, their family already had a daughter. Sakiko's father had made it clear—he wanted a boy! So when my wife was born, he was very disappointed. To make matters worse, Sakiko's father, like many men of his generation in Japan, was often absent from the home due to his work. My wife grew up with a profound sense that she wasn't wanted by her father.

Not long after she gave her life to Christ as a young adult, Sakiko sensed God saying something to her. She heard God speaking to her heart, saying "You are Isaac." She didn't understand why she was being named Isaac, so she began reading the story of Isaac in the Bible, and she learned that he was a promised child, one who was deeply wanted by his elderly parents, Abraham and Sarah, because they had been infertile for decades. As she read Isaac's story, she felt God saying to her: "You are a desired, promised child." This word of affirmation has remained with her over the years, and has helped her to realize how deeply she is loved by God.

Sometime later, Sakiko discovered Paul's words in Galatians 4:28, confirming that those who belong to Christ are the "children of promise." And that word isn't just for my wife—it's true for all of us. If you have surrendered your life to God, you have been adopted into God's family. You too are Isaac. You are a child of Abraham. You are deeply wanted and cherished by a perfect Father in heaven. Through God's love, Sakiko was freed from her sense of deprivation and need to prove her worth as she lived into her new identity as a *child of grace*. And this can be true for you as well!

> *If you have surrendered your life to God, you have been adopted into God's family. You are Isaac. You are deeply wanted and cherished by a perfect Father in heaven.*

Several years ago, I was invited to speak in Fukushima and Sendai, Japan, cities that were devastated by the massive tsunami that hit Japan on March 11, 2011. While there, I encountered the music of Solnamoo Song, a man who spent the early years of his life in Korea where his father served as president of a company. After the company went bankrupt, his father urged the rest of the family to move to the US, thinking they would have better prospects there. Solnamoo's father chose to remain behind in Korea to seek out work.

Solnamoo and the rest of his family moved into his uncle's small two-bedroom home on the East Coast. Other extended family members moved in, and eventually fourteen people were crammed into that tiny home! Their extended family was poor and they could not even afford a television. Even if they had been able to pay for one, there would have been no place to put it!

Solnamoo's older sister Min was very intelligent and unusually talented, and her work was eventually recognized by President George H. W. Bush, who gave her an award. Solnamoo felt like nothing compared to his sister. Whenever it was necessary to acknowledge Solnamoo to a new person, his mother would refer to him as "Min's younger brother." He felt like a nobody. And his experiences at school only confirmed that lie. As a ten-year-old Korean boy who spoke broken English, Solnamoo was regularly teased and beaten up at school. He would spend his lunch hours hiding in a toilet stall.

One day while hiding, with tears streaming down his cheeks, he cried out: "Why is life so unfair? Why can't I be smart and loved by my mom like my older sister? I'm a mistake!"

To his surprise, Solnamoo heard a clear voice respond.

"You're not a mistake. You're my son and I love you. I know things about you that even your mother does not know. I know the number of hairs you have on your head." Then he heard the voice summon him, "Come out of the toilet!"

Solnamoo's head snapped back, and he stepped out of the stall. At that moment he was filled with a fresh realization that he was truly loved by God. As he marched down the hall of the school with newfound confidence, he heard music playing. The school band happened to be practicing in the band room, and Solnamoo walked into the rehearsal. The conductor saw him standing there and asked him to join the band.

Until that day, Solnamoo had very little experience with music. He had taken a handful of flute lessons in Korea but could only play *do-re-me-fa-so-la-ti*. Normally, because of his shame, he would have declined an invitation to step out and risk rejection. But filled with a profound new sense of being loved by his Maker, he said yes instead. The conductor handed him a flute, and Solnamoo began to blow into it.

After several months of practicing the flute, it became apparent to his teacher that Solnamoo had a gift. At the age of thirteen, lacking any formal training, Solnamoo applied to the pre-college program at the Juilliard School of Music in New York City. Standing in line for the audition, he learned that the well-dressed applicant in front of him was the daughter of the president of a famous company. Her flute was priceless. She made sure he knew that she'd had the very best music teachers growing up.

Feeling self-conscious with his secondhand flute, held together by tape, Solnamoo nervously stepped onto the stage before a panel of professors and music experts. He played for them. When he finished, they huddled together, laughing and whispering to each other. With a smirk, one of them turned to Solnamoo and asked, "Why are you auditioning with such a cheap, old instrument?"

"This is the only flute I can afford," Solnamoo replied.

A week later he received a letter from Juilliard. He had been admitted to the school, and he was being given a scholarship.

Solnamoo would go on to perform at the Lincoln Center, Carnegie Hall, and prestigious venues around the world. But he never forgot the root of all his success—the knowledge that he was loved by God. In gratitude for that gift of grace, he has performed many free concerts in the cities of Fukushima and Sendai. Why? Having been blessed he now longs to bless others by bringing beauty and comfort to those who have suffered.

Most people are driven to perform *in order to* earn respect and win the love of others. And there is nothing wrong with hard work. But the beauty and joy of Solnamoo's music is not rooted in his desire to achieve recognition. It flows from the deeper knowledge that he is already respected and loved by God his Father. He is not a slave to success; he is a child of grace.*

From Seeking Approval to Accepting our Acceptance

Like Sakiko and Solnamoo, I too have experienced this same awareness of God's profound love for me. I've sensed it as a new follower of Jesus, while standing alone at a bus stop, in the wake of a painful breakup, and at the birth of our child. But my memory is short, and there are many days when I forget that I am loved. I find myself wanting to succeed for all the wrong reasons. When I look into my heart I see that I want to do great things to win the respect of other people. And if I use my gifts I can often achieve success. But it's like a drug—I find that I need a bigger hit every time to satisfy the desire. Is there hope for those of us addicted to our success and the driving need for approval?

The great theologian Paul Tillich tells us that "we must *accept* the fact that we are accepted." And I love that in the margin of his sermon notes, he added, "This is for me."

Do you accept the fact that you are accepted?

Do you claim your belovedness?

---

* Solnamoo's story also shows us that a deep experience of God's love can awaken both a dormant Striving Adam and a sleeping Soulful Adam.

Do you live as a daughter or son of grace?

You may be saying to yourself, *I want to. But how do I do this? How do I accept the fact that I am accepted?*

In my experience, I've found that

Do you live as a daughter or son of grace?

my awareness of grace—of a love that I can't earn and don't deserve—has deepened as I have embraced spiritual practices that create space for God in my life. These life-giving habits leave me feeling less restless, more comfortable in my own skin. I'm stirred to contribute out of deep gratitude for the grace I have been given, rather than out of my need to validate myself. As the Holy Spirit works in me through these habits, I am freed to live *from* approval instead of *for* approval.

It is true that God is with us all the time. He is reaching out to us each day through people in our lives, by creation, and Scripture. He speaks in moments of beauty, through our memories and desires.

Sadly, most of us remain distracted and unaware.

This is why the habit of spiritual practices is so essential to our soul's survival. The practices we will learn about in this book awaken us to God's presence, enabling us to live freely out of our new identity as beloved children of God. And as we become more attentive to God's abiding presence in our lives, labels such as *stupid, mistake, fraud, not enough, worthless, ugly,* and *loser* fall away. They are replaced by other words. Words of truth, spoken by the one who made us.

Beloved.

Beautiful.

Blessed.

Questions *for* Reflection and Discussion

———————◇———————

1. Were you able to relate to Augustine's inner wrestling? Are you tempted by fame or success as a way to validate your existence?
2. Do you know someone like Ken's mother or Leighton Ford, whose ambitions were transformed by God?
3. Do you ever worry that your life doesn't measure up? If so, whose expectations do you worry that you won't meet?
4. How do you feel when you hear that God has already accepted you and you have nothing to prove? Do you find this difficult to believe?
5. What helps you feel loved by God?
6. What blocks you from feeling loved?
7. How could you become less of a slave to success and more of a child of grace?

Prayer

Abba, Father, thank you for making me your cherished child. Train my heart to enjoy our relationship. Send your Spirit to help my heart believe the sweet truth that I am embraced. Make my adoption a reality that governs my thoughts, feelings, and actions.[11]

Chapter 3

SPIRITUAL PRACTICES

*The disciplines allow us to place ourselves before God
so He can transform us.*[1]

–RICHARD FOSTER

I tend to be forgetful. So if I need to remember to buy milk on the way home from work, I put a sticky note on my wallet to remind me. Then, when I get to the office, I put another sticky note with the word *milk* on the seat of my bicycle. (Yes, I really am that forgetful.)

It's easy to forget God—especially if we're busy and enjoy accomplishing things. We grow used to living from task to task, craving the dopamine hit that comes from the next big thing.

We forget that there is an alternative to this way of life. Spiritual exercises attune us to God's presence, acting as sticky-note reminders that *God is with us all the time.* They don't lift us high into God's atmosphere, like jet propulsion helps launch a plane thirty thousand feet above the ground. We're *already* in God's presence. Rather, the practices tune us into the invisible waves of God's

> *Spiritual exercises attune us to God's presence, acting as sticky-note reminders that* God is with us all the time.

loving presence in whom we live and move and have our being (Acts 17:28). The exercises don't offer merely a fleeting high. They foster the deeper joy of a steady, solid relationship of love.

Reminders of Whose We Are

In the movie *50 First Dates,* Drew Barrymore's character gets in a car accident and suffers brain trauma. The injury causes a rare amnesia that resets her memory every time she goes to sleep at night. Her boyfriend, played by Adam Sandler, takes her on fifty "first dates," trying to convince her over time that they belong to each other and to help her remember that they're in love. Individually, the dates, no matter how outrageous and amazingly planned, don't succeed. So he produces a video to remind her of their story—and as she watches the video over and over every morning, she slowly remembers that she is loved by Sandler and loves him in return.

Like Barrymore's character, we easily forget that we are deeply loved by our Maker. A rhythm of spiritual practices helps us remember to whom we belong and by whom we are loved.

Reminders of Who We Are

Our hearts actually can be trained to live with an ongoing awareness that we are loved by God. While this may sound rather abstract, it's really very practical. We can live day to day with a real relational presence in our lives that will profoundly affect the way we travel through the world. When we know we are loved, we move through life *bolder* because we fear failure less. For instance, I (who am naturally terrified of failure) can push the boat of this imperfect book into the waters of the world knowing that even if it's shot down and sinks, I'll be okay because I'm *already* accepted. When we know we are held by an unconditional love, and we fail, we won't drown in self-loathing; we will have the buoyancy to swim on.

When we succeed we will recognize our success as an expression of God's grace, and paradoxically, we will grow more confident *and* humble.

Many of us—even those of us who intellectually believe that God is love—have difficulty truly believing that *we* are loved.

As simple as the words sound, many of us cannot easily "accept the fact that I am accepted."

The perceptive priest Henri Nouwen observes that the greatest temptation we face is self-rejection. He says it's not sex, popularity, or power. Those seductions are very real, but there is usually a deeper dynamic at work. Our quest for sex, popularity, or power are often rooted in a deeper longing for acceptance and respect. Self-rejection is the greatest temptation because it contradicts the sacred voice that calls us the beloved.[2] And being the beloved is the core truth of our existence.

Practices that Help Us Feel Loved and Whole

The practices open the ear of our spirit to hear the sacred voice that calls us the beloved. They enlighten the eyes of our heart to accept this core truth of our existence.

When we are standing on a literal (or metaphorical) mountaintop, listening to gorgeous music, holding a newborn baby, or seeing a door of opportunity swing open for us, we can easily feel awash in God's love. But the intensity of these feelings is fleeting. Spiritual practices train our heart to grow *continually conscious of* the core truth that we are beloved of God. We may have had a powerful "conversion" experience in the past, but because of our spiritual amnesia we need to awaken to God's love every day and be born again and again and again. As we open ourselves to the Holy Spirit through the spiritual disciplines, Christ's love is birthed and rebirthed in us.

As this happens, like Barrymore's character, we are reminded of the one to whom we belong and by whom are loved. And as we live in the fullness of God's love for us, we are made new (Ephesians 3:14–19; 2 Corinthians 5:17).

But what does this actually look like in the day-to-day of our busy lives? In what follows, I want to introduce you briefly to some of the spiritual habits that are especially relevant for those of us who tend to *define ourselves by what we do*. In the chapters to come, we'll take a deeper dive into each one of these essential habits of the soul.

Silent Meditation

When you get up in the morning, what's the first thing you do? If you are like most people, you may feel the pressure to pick up your phone and check for texts, email, or the latest news. The introduction of the smartphone into our lives in the past decade has changed us in ways we are only beginning to understand.

What do I do when I wake up in the morning? Well, for starters, I make a conscious choice *not* to check my email, text messages, or the internet. Are these things inherently bad or wrong? No. But I know they will get my mind racing in different directions, and my thinking will quickly become dominated by my "to do" list. So I avoid my phone.

Instead, at the beginning of the day, I choose to do things that help me attend to God's presence. As I will describe in more detail in chapter four, I begin each morning by sitting and breathing deeply for fifteen or twenty minutes. I find that this practice helps to still my busy brain.

I also find that holding a phrase or a single word from Scripture, such as "be still" (Psalm 46:10) or "wait" (Isaiah 40:31), helps focus my distracted thoughts on God and primes me to notice his loving presence throughout the day. Just as physical exercise in the morning lifts my mood and permeates the rest of my waking hours, the simple practice of morning meditation helps me to become more mindful of God's compassionate eye watching over me as the day unfolds.

Although God is with us all the time, so often we are unaware of his presence. A simple rhythm of morning meditation or pausing at brief moments in the day to attend to God nurtures our awareness of his love for us, even when we are not consciously praying.

Sabbath Keeping

Even as a child I had a strong Striving Adam work orientation (except when I was supposed to be studying for school!). At the age of ten, I started working as a newspaper delivery boy for the *Vancouver Sun*, the largest daily newspaper in our region. By the age of thirteen, I had become the newspaper depot manager and was overseeing the kids who were delivering newspapers. During my twenties, I typically began my workday (including the commute) at seven in the morning and didn't get home until past eleven at night. When I began pastoring I found that I was easily clocking seventy hours of work each week.

I tend to define myself by what I do and how well I do it. But over time and by God's grace, I have learned to break this pattern of making what I *do* the central part of my identity. And one of the most powerful ways to do this might surprise you. It's by honoring the Sabbath.

As I explore in chapter five, honoring the Sabbath helps me become more aware of God's love for me because it reminds me that *my value doesn't come from what I produce* but from the fact that I am loved by a perfect Father in heaven. If you are a parent, you know how you love a newborn baby *before* the child accomplishes anything of significance in the world. At Jesus' baptism, *before* he ever preached a sermon, healed a single person, or achieved anything noteworthy, his Father said, "This is my beloved Son, in whom I am well pleased" (Matthew 3:17 KJV).

God says the same to you. *Before* you have done anything noteworthy, he calls you his beloved.

When we cease working on our Sabbath, we *live* out the truth that our worth is not based on how much we accomplish or contribute to the world but on the simple glorious fact that we are a cherished child of God. This awareness of God's love mediated through practices like silent meditation or the Sabbath not only satisfies Soulful Adam's yearning for connection with our Maker but also helps Striving Adam to flourish. When our Striving Adam operates from a place of belovedness, we can take risks without a paralyzing fear of failure. We can offer our *best* not out of a fretful need to prove ourselves but from a swell of gratitude and joy.

Living loved helps Soulful Adam come alive and brings out the best in Striving Adam.

Practices that Cultivate Humility

Those of us who determine our value based on what we do are inclined to feel that we aren't good enough. We tend to compare ourselves to people who seem to be accomplishing more than us.

We thus need practices that remind us how much we are loved. Those of us who are "doers" are, ironically, also prone to see ourselves as superior to others. We might look down on those who are less productive than we are, or lack formal education, or who are less (or more) progressive in their social views. The antidote? We embrace the practices that help us to grow more humble and less self-absorbed.

Gratitude

As we'll discover in chapter six, taking time each day to notice and give thanks for specific things helps us to become conscious of the good in our lives. In the evening, I will regularly pause, look back over the day, and list at least three things for which I am thankful. These expressions of gratitude may be as simple as thanking God for a pleasurable run on a crisp morning with our golden retriever, a meaningful conversation with someone, and a cozy home and comfortable bed in which to sleep. When I associate these gifts with God's goodness, I become more conscious of God's great love for me. My eyes are opened to the reality that I haven't pulled myself up by my bootstraps, but I am what I am and I have what I have because of the sheer grace of God. *Gratitude births humility.*

Servanthood

In chapter eight we'll see that when we serve others, we are reminded that *we do not exist for our own personal glory or fulfillment but for the honor of God and benefit of others.* When we serve, we also discover that our most important calling is almost always lived out in the ordinary tasks of everyday life.

When my friend Zack was in seminary, everyone agreed that he would be successful, perhaps even famous one day. As a new pastor, he wrote two books in three years, and one of them won a national award. One day, while he was driving home after speaking at a conference, he received a phone call from his wife of fifteen years. "I can no longer be married to you," she said. "I no longer consider myself a Christian. I never loved you, and I'm now in love with someone else." Zack was heartbroken. In addition to the pain of the broken marriage, he knew that his ministry days were over. The message of his books was now tainted by his failed marriage, and even though he was declared innocent by church leaders in the subsequent divorce, the scandal and gossip that swirled around him forced him to step down from the pastorate.

As he switched roles to focus on being the primary caregiver for his three young children, Zack began to ask himself, "If I am no longer a pastor, do I still have value as a person? If I never preach again, will Jesus still love me? If the most important tasks of my day are changing a diaper or preparing meals for my three young children, will my life still be important? If I am serving in

ordinary ways as an ordinary human being, will my life matter?"
As Zack sought God in prayer, he heard Jesus saying the same
thing, over and over.

Yes. Yes. Yes.

Today, Zack has returned to public ministry. He is writing
books again, and he has become a sought-after speaker. But his
heart has changed. He has been apprenticed with Jesus through
the humble service of loving his children in the obscurity of his
home. Even though he works hard in his church ministry (and
on the home front), he is no longer driven to seek status and
fame. Jesus has taught him the humble mindset of a servant. His
reordered heart reflects different priorities, and he is now a man
who is at peace with himself.

When we choose to practice the discipline of service—
whether it's preparing family meals, coaching our children's
soccer team, visiting inmates at the local jail, or engaging our
paid employment with a servant mindset—we walk the path of
the servant. We crucify our selfish, hollow ambitions—putting
in motion a death that is often painful. Jesus never promised following in his footsteps would be easy, but the truth is that when
we serve others we are pursuing a beautiful countercultural
greatness. Jesus wants to teach us his way of life: how to live
justly, love mercy, and walk humbly with our God (Micah 6:8).
Having the Christlike mindset of a servant (Philippians 2:5)
satisfies our Soulful Adam's longing to love and serve others. But
it also unleashes Striving Adam's passion to make a difference
in the world.

Whether we are called to raise children or lead a major cor-
poration (or both!), our soul will be healthier, our world a better
place, and God will be honored if we offer our very best with

a hardnosed Striving Adam resolve *and* a wide-eyed Soulful Adam humility. Spiritual disciplines open our lives to the ocean of God's love. They make us more confident and humble, transforming us into the complete people we are created and called to be.

Embracing Practices that Sustain Us

Although practices such as silent prayer or serving may sound demanding (and they can be), we should not think of them as a duty-driven grind. Like anything worthwhile, spiritual training is moving us toward a goal that is in harmony with the way we were made to live. This means that we need to embrace the spiritual practices that are *consistent with the grain of our character.* Ideally, these practices will meet our deepest joy and our deepest need. As with physical exercise, if our spiritual exercises are life-giving, they will become sustainable and even enjoyable over time.

> *As with physical exercise, if our spiritual exercises are life-giving, they will become sustainable and even enjoyable over time.*

I enjoy running, but not on a treadmill. Still, when I'm traveling to a place like Boston in the dead of winter with a foot of snow on the ground, I don't run outside. I use the treadmill, even though I don't like it. It's a temporary measure for special circumstances. But if I had to use that machine every day as my *primary* way to exercise, I don't know that I would stick with it. The treadmill doesn't align with who I am. I know other people who are the opposite: they love that machine! Based on our unique constitution, certain exercises will be more natural for us, a better fit for who we are. In the same way, some spiritual practices will prove more suitable and fruitful for us than others.

A study of people with different kinds of temperaments (as defined by the Myers-Briggs personality profile) examined each temperament's preferred spiritual practices, using several historical Catholic teachers to embody various spiritual "languages of love."[3] The research found that around 40 percent of people in North America are "Ignatian" in their spirituality. This means that their approach to God is similar to Saint Ignatius of Loyola, a sixteenth-century follower of Jesus. *Ignatian* types are very practical, have a strong sense of responsibility, and love to serve in tangible ways, such as preparing a meal for someone who is ill, or hammering a nail in the frame of the house they are helping to build with a Habitat for Humanity team. These tasks make them feel like they are doing something useful. They like organization and structure. They also tend to prefer a more consistent, ordered approach to God.

Roughly 38 percent of the population is "Franciscan" in their approach to spirituality. Like St. Francis of Assisi, a fourteenth-century lover of God and creation, *Franciscan* types connect most deeply with God as they walk in nature, enjoy beautiful art or music, listen to inspiring stories, or savor a cup of coffee and good conversation with a friend. Rather than favoring structure, they tend to prefer a more spontaneous approach to God.

About 12 percent of the population is "Augustinian" in their spirituality. They resemble St. Augustine, the brilliant thinker and leader who lived in the fourth and fifth centuries. *Augustinian* types are philosophical and enjoy contemplating the meaning of God and their lives. Although just over one in ten people have this Augustinian approach to God, they may represent more than 50 percent of those who schedule time to get away on spiritual retreats.

Only 10 percent of the population tends to be "Thomistic" in their approach to God. Their spirituality is similar to St. Thomas Aquinas, a towering theologian from the thirteenth century. *Thomistics* love to use their minds as a gateway to God. They relish the study of Scripture, theology, and substantive Christian books. A disproportionately high percentage of pastors, in comparison with the general population, are *Thomistic* in their spirituality. This helps explain why many pastors frequently stress the importance of Bible study and theological learning as a way for people to grow in their faith.

Even though I am a pastor and have deep convictions about the importance of Bible study, I recognize that there are various ways for people to connect with God. For some people, in certain seasons of life, studying the Bible or theology in depth may not be the *primary* way to encounter God, and it's not helpful to experience unnecessary guilt about that. For all of us, it is important that we find the particular spiritual practices that are life-giving because they are consistent with who we are. We want to embrace what is most fruitful in helping us grow in our love for God and others based on where we are on our spiritual journey.

If you are new to either physical *or* spiritual exercise, here's a user-warning alert: it may take a little experimentation and patience to see if a particular practice will bear fruit! When I convinced my former roommate, Mike, who had never spent time running before, to go on a jog with me one morning, I assured him he would feel energized afterward. At the end of our jog, I asked, "How are you feeling?" Mike bowled over, clutching his stomach. "I feel like puking," he said. I assured him that he would feel more energy throughout the day, so when he came home from work that evening, I asked him about his day. "I was so tired, I could hardly concentrate," he said. Later in life, I learned that it takes about thirty or forty days for a person to feel the benefits of exercise, the increased alertness and energy that I had naively promised him on the first day.

We must remember that spiritual practices may feel challenging at first but often eventually prove life-giving. For example, when we begin to practice silent meditative prayer, we may become discouraged by distractions. We may struggle with random thoughts invading our mind. It takes time and practice before we will feel centered and rooted through silence. When we first learn to tithe (giving away at least 10 percent of our income to God's work in the world), or begin observing Sabbath rest, we may struggle at first. But over time these practices can bring us into a place of great freedom and even joy. As is true with any endeavor, discerning whether a spiritual practice is going to be sustainable and fruitful will take trial and error along with perseverance.

Practices Shape How We Inhabit Our World

We don't engage in spiritual practices to check off a list and appease a distorted Striving Adam compulsion. That may lead to spiritual pride, which is hazardous for the soul. Instead, with God's help we embrace spiritual practices that shape the way we move through the world.

Some days, I feel as if nothing is going right for me. I face scathing criticism. A talk flounders. It looks like we are falling perilously behind our financial targets. On these days, I wonder if our church would be better off with another leader. My self-esteem free-falls. Then there are other days when I receive a lot of praise, or our Sunday worship attendance swells. On these days, I feel smug. I'm "the man"—our church and city are fortunate to have me!

Wallowing in self-doubt and indulging our pride are both unhealthy. On the days when I am tempted to despair, the habits of spiritual practices remind me that no matter what crashes in my life, I remain a beloved child of God. I'm filled with the confidence and courage to march on. And on those days when I am tempted to exult in my triumphs, the spiritual disciplines reset my gratitude meter, enabling me to live with a deeper sense of wonder, awe, and humility at the goodness of God. Engaging spiritual practices helps me inhabit the world in a healthy way by freeing me to live from the best parts of myself. In the following chapters, we'll delve into the survival habits of the soul that awaken us to God's love and empower us to live with confidence and humility.

Questions *for* Reflection and Discussion

◆

1. What practices might help you remember that you are loved by God?
2. How do spiritual disciplines help to cultivate humility?
3. Can you identify a particular vulnerability that you might have? Is there a spiritual practice that might help prevent the "house" of your life from being burned?
4. In light of your temperament, are there one or two spiritual practices that would be especially life-giving for you?
5. If you feel that you are failing in a particular practice, how might you respond in a grace-filled, constructive way?

Prayer

Lord, through the gift of my spiritual practices, help me to open to the work of your Holy Spirit so that I can become the masterpiece you are creating me to be.

–SEE EPHESIANS 2:10

PART 2

THE SURVIVAL HABITS OF
the Soul

Chapter 4

MEDITATION

Listening to the Music of Heaven

*We all must take time to be silent and to contemplate,
especially those of us who live in big cities . . . where
everything moves so fast. . . . I always begin my
prayer in silence, for it is in the silence of the heart
that God speaks.*[1]

–MOTHER TERESA

When I first started working at the church where I pastor, if I'd had a very full, stressful day, I'd eat a late dinner while vegging out in front of the TV. It helped me to relax. The first show I'd tune into would entertain me, but by the end of that two-hour television binge, I'd feel even more restless than before. I've now changed my habits. I've learned that the best thing I can do after a hard day at work is to go on a bike ride with my son or take our golden retriever on a run. These things "take the edge off" my stress in a way that sitting in front of a television cannot.

According to psychologist Dr. Anne Wilson-Schaef, 98 percent of us are addicted to something that helps us cope with life.[2] I've never met anyone in the other 2 percent! In his book

Addiction and Grace, Dr. Gerald May, a respected psychiatrist and spiritual director, contends that one hundred percent of us are addicted to something. Yes, 100 percent. Yet most of us don't see ourselves as "addicts."

Interestingly, May points out that the word "addiction" comes from the old French word *attaché*, a reference to a junior member of the government who is *attached* to an ambassador or another high-ranking official.[3] I find that word picture helpful. When we get addicted to something, it's as if we've *attached* ourselves to it relationally. We attach ourselves for many reasons, often to numb our pain or lessen the boredom or meaninglessness of our lives. Some people turn to television, alcohol, or food for comfort. Others seek solace in a relationship, sexual activity, social media, shopping, or pushing the limits of physical endurance. If you are reading this book you may be seeking consolation in your work or some kind of achievement right now. Overachieving is a common way we try to numb our sense of not being enough.

Sometimes we are addicted or attached to things that aren't necessarily bad in and of themselves, such as exercise or work. But if we cannot say no to something, then we have an addiction. The thing we've attached ourselves to has control over us in some way. If we cannot say no to work for twenty-four hours in order to embrace the Sabbath, we are addicted to our work. We are its *attaché*, and we've lost our freedom. An addiction disrupts and displaces God as the center of our lives, and the Bible has a word for this: idolatry.

Countless people who have gone through the twelve-step program of Alcoholics Anonymous say that one of the most powerful ways to overcome an addiction is step eleven: cultivating the practices of "prayer and meditation to improve our conscious contact with God." Prayer is commonly understood as speaking to God and meditation involves quietly savoring God's presence. In meditation and silent prayer, our posture is *receptive* rather than expressive, *attentive* rather than spoken.

Stillness and Movement

In Psalm 46, God says, "Be still, and know that I am God" (v. 10).

Job prayed, "Teach me, and I will be quiet" (6:24).

In Exodus, God calls his people to trust that he will fight on their behalf: "The LORD will fight for you; you need only to be still" (14:14).

In the midst of a demanding ministry, Jesus pursued silence and solitude in "a solitary place" to hear the Father's voice (Luke 4:42).

Though at times we are called to engage in battle against the "enemies within," such as vanity, anger, lust, greed, and envy, often we are called to be still before the Lord, waiting and watching for his transforming work within us. In the twenty-third psalm, God calls us (literally or figuratively) to lie down in green pastures and rest beside quiet waters in order to restore our souls. As the presence of the great Shepherd frees our hearts from anxiety and pain, we are less likely to turn to an addiction for comfort because our heart finds rest in God.

But sometimes being "still" before God doesn't mean being *literally* still. Sometimes it means moving.

John Cassian, the great spiritual father of the fifth century, instructed the monks under his care to weave baskets while praying and meditating because he understood that sometimes a simple physical movement fosters a greater stillness of our mind. Depending on our "wiring" and temperament, some of us may find that if we're simply sitting still, trying to focus on one thing, random thoughts come crashing into our minds. For some people, a focused activity can help still their mind—such as taking a drive down a long stretch of road with few traffic lights or other cars, walking, knitting, or making bread.

In a beautiful book on contemplation, *Into the Silent Land*, Martin Laird describes a woman who harbored deep pain from her childhood. When she was a young girl, she was sitting in her bedroom looking at herself in the mirror, and her mother walked down the hallway. Seeing her daughter through the open door, the mother shouted at her, "I hope you don't think you're beautiful." Even though this young girl was quite beautiful by any outward standard, she started to believe she was ugly. As a teenager she won a prestigious scholarship to study ballet, and again her mother criticized her. "Why would they give you that? Everybody knows you've got two left feet." She went on to become a celebrated dancer, performing to thunderous applause around the world, but deep inside she continued to believe that she was an ugly klutz with two left feet.

As an adult living in England, this woman found peace by taking long walks across the Yorkshire moors. If she walked long enough, she found that her mind began to settle. The expanse of scented heather was a balm that soothed her internal anger, fear, and pain. On one occasion, she felt her anxiety drop from her, like shedding off layers of scarves, and she became acutely aware of being immersed in a holy, loving presence that upheld her in everything. Although this experience happened just once, it was a mystical turning point in her life, drawing her more deeply into the way of prayer.[4] It was a healing moment in which she became profoundly aware of God's love and acceptance.

Here in Vancouver, I have a friend who struggles with depression. Each morning, he goes on a slow walk through his neighborhood. Walking silently helps to keep his depression at bay as he becomes more conscious of God. Both the ballet dancer and my Vancouver friend have experienced what St. Augustine calls *solvitur ambulando*: "It is solved by walking."

For some, walking is a way of being still before the Lord while for others, being still before the Lord means sitting in God's presence. The posture of sitting serves as a powerful symbol of our desire to be still. For those of us with a strong Striving Adam, we may feel like our world will come crashing down if we're not spinning it constantly with our hand, keeping everything in motion. For us, sitting may also serve as a physical reminder that the world moves by God's hand, not our own. As we sit, we are saying with our posture that we are waiting in faith for God to act. Sitting silently can also invite our shy Soulful Adam to step out of the shadows and begin to influence our lives.

Attention

In prayer, we don't *invoke* God's presence—for God is with us all the time. Meditation helps us to become more aware of the God who is already with us. Simone Weil, the French mystic, describes prayer as *attention*. Silent prayer leads to a powerful change in the way we inhabit the world because it grows our capacity to pay attention to our Creator, even when we are not *consciously* praying.

Each morning before breakfast, I take time to sit quietly and meditate in God's presence. To begin, I breathe deeply, inhaling and exhaling through my nose. Then I light a candle to symbolize the light of Christ's presence. After a few moments, I begin to wonder, "How much time has gone by?" To focus, I use an app on my phone called "Centering Prayer," which has a timer. Often I set it for twenty minutes, but sometimes I set it for ten or fifteen minutes. The app has a chime that summons me to attend to God like a bell in a monastery. I am so easily distracted that not long after taking a couple of deep breaths, I usually start thinking of all the things I *ought* to be doing. To still my mind, I focus on a brief portion of Scripture, such as the phrase from Psalm 46:*

> *Silent prayer leads to a powerful change in the way we inhabit the world because it grows our capacity to pay attention to our Creator, even when we are not consciously praying.*

Breathe in.

"Be still."

Breathe out.

"Know that I am God."

Breathe in.

"Be still."

Breathe out.

"Know that I am God."

---

* I have also found it helpful to prime my mind for meditation by using a devotional guide such as *Seeking God's Face* by Phil Reinders, designed to help us meditate on brief portions of Scripture. Or the *Pray as You Go* website that plays beautiful sacred music and then offers a brief imaginative guide through a passage of Scripture. If I feel unusually distracted, I breathe in and out, focus on my breathing and start counting breaths from 1 to 10. As I inhale, I will count an odd number and as I exhale I will count an even number. I count only to 10 and then repeat the sequence.

Sometimes I use a single word from Scripture, such as "wait" (Isaiah 40), to help me focus on God.

Breathe in.

"Wait."

Breathe out.

"Wait."

Jesus warned against vain repetition in Matthew 6:7, but there is nothing *vain* about gently calling ourselves to be still before God. There is nothing hollow about focusing on a word such as "love" to remind us of the love of the Father, or centering on the name "Jesus" or simply "God."

The Four Guidelines to Centering Prayer[5]

1. Choose a sacred word as the symbol of your intention to consent to God's presence and action within.
2. Sitting comfortably, with a straight spine and eyes closed, settle briefly. Silently introduce the sacred word as the symbol of your consent to God's presence and action within.
3. As your thoughts* engage you, return gently to the sacred word.
4. At the end of the prayer period, remain in silence with eyes closed for a couple of minutes.

---

* Thoughts include body sensations, feelings, images, and reflections.

I love being on the water, and I like to compare meditation to sailing. Sometimes I see garbage floating on the surface of the ocean: plastic bags, a Coke can, or wooden debris. Other times I see salmon jumping out of the water, seals, pods of dolphins, and, on rare occasions, even whales.

As we sit quietly in God's presence and relax, garbage may rise to the surface on the sea of our lives—anxiety, fear, disappointment, resentment, envy, pain, shame, or anger. When we offer this garbage up to God, we experience purging and cleansing. Though this garbage may return, we offer it up to God again and experience new freedom.

But other times, we may receive the gift of being quietly surrounded by the holy, loving mysterious presence that upholds us and the whole world. Most people do not experience anything particularly dramatic during meditation. Meditation is rather ordinary most of the time. Nonetheless, I find that the best way to begin the day is to be still and remember that God is God, and I am not.

A Life Rhythm

Steve is a single dad in our faith community. He has two young children and a demanding job that requires him to travel regularly. Steve shared with me recently that each morning he tries to do a little stretching and meditating—just ten minutes or so. When I asked if it made a difference in his life, he said, "Oh, yes. When I meditate, God shows up more during the day."

Obviously, God does not "show up" more, because God is with Steve all the time. But when Steve meditates in the morning, he is more *aware* of the God who is always with him. Of course, we can "pray as we go," but when we set aside a regular time for God, the eyes of our heart are primed to notice God more throughout the day. Father Thomas Keating, a well-known author on Christian meditation, points out that spiritual practices are designed to reduce the monumental illusion that God is absent.[6]

Meditation also shapes the way we relate to ourselves, our work, and other people. When Andrew, an engineer who is easily distracted, began to experiment with meditation, he assumed that the goal of meditation was to empty his mind. As he tried to focus on his breathing, other thoughts leaked into his brain. Feeling like a terrible meditator, he was ready to give up because he sensed he was wasting his time. But as he reflected on his experience, Andrew realized that though he was distracted during his ten or twenty minutes of meditation, he was more focused on the days he meditated than on the days when he skipped it. He noticed that on the days he meditated and wanted to order something deep-fried and salty (he was trying to watch his diet), he was more likely to make a healthier eating choice. He noticed that when he meditated, he was more likely to bite his tongue when he had a sarcastic comment on his lips. And he realized that on the days he mediated, when he became distracted at work, he was able to refocus and get back on track more quickly.[7] Meditation for Andrew helped satiate a Soulful Adam yearning for connection, but also fulfilled a Striving Adam desire to focus while working.

Meditation is also practical. Dr. Kelly McGonigal, a psychologist who teaches at Stanford, points out that if you meditate for as little as ten or fifteen minutes a day over three weeks, you will show signs of greater attention and self-control. If you meditate for as little as ten to fifteen minutes a day for two to three months, an MRI scan on your brain would show that the neural networks in your brain associated with being able to focus and control your impulses has actually grown, and the gray matter in your head associated with feeling anxiety and depression has actually shrunk.[8]

My friend Carol, a mother of young children and a social worker, practiced daily meditation for three months, but because of her demanding schedule she couldn't sustain this practice at the same time each day. Carol, however, discovered she could practice meditation at various moments in her day. She shares:

I am a busy working mom balancing two part-time jobs and two [young] kids. I have always valued having a schedule and doing things at a predictable time, and I felt like if it [mediation] didn't happen before 10:30 p.m. it was "too late." Mornings are out for me, because of our kids and the busyness of our routine. One thing I discovered is that I could go "off schedule" and engage in some meditation in the middle of my day! Literally between patients or clients, I would give myself five to ten minutes, close my office door and practice, or I would wait outside one of the kid's lessons and practice in the car. It is extremely centering and reenergizing, and clarifies what used to be the haziest part of my day. I think just because of my nature, I will always be a busy person—but I no longer feel like I have a busy mind!

As Carol and countless others affirm, taking even five or ten minutes in our day to meditate can bring a greater sense of calm and clarity to our life.

The goal of meditation is not to experience bliss in a singular moment. Rather it is to rest in our Father's company and to consent to the work of the Holy Spirit in every aspect of our lives. As we wait on God, we may feel distracted and even bored, but over time we will become more aware that God is with us—especially during the parts of the day when we are *not consciously praying.*

The goal of meditation is not to become a "successful meditator," but to open our soul, mind, and body to the quiet work of the Holy Spirit so that we become more attentive to God's movements within and around us. Just as physically exercising for a day won't make a difference in our health, meditating for a day won't create any lasting changes for us. But if we incorporate meditation into the rhythm of our lives, it will transform our way of being in the world.

> *Though taking ten or twenty minutes to meditate may seem like a self-indulgent luxury, without it we will only have our distracted, depleted selves to offer.*

Though taking ten or twenty minutes to meditate may seem like a self-indulgent luxury, without it we will only have our distracted, depleted selves to offer. A practice that centers us, refreshes us, and enables us to offer more of ourselves to God and others is wise stewardship of the only gift—the gift of ourselves—that we have to offer the world.[9]

In the Presence of
the Divine Archaeologist

Imagine you are an archaeology student on an excavation dig somewhere in the Middle East. As you explore, you come across a mound called a tell.

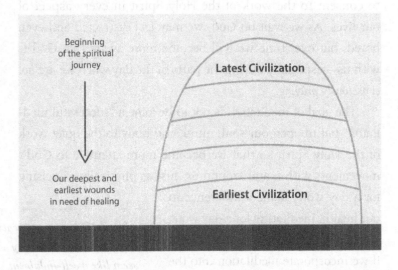

In ancient times, when a city-state defeated one of its enemies, the military would burn down the rival city and build a new city on top of the old one. In turn, when that city-state was defeated, its conquerors would build a new city on top of it, and so on. Today, when we dig at that location we find one civilization built on top of another. When archaeologists are working on one of these sites, their first job is to clean off the top and get rid of the rocks and weeds. They then unearth the civilization that once thrived there. After sending the uncovered pottery and tools to a museum, the team returns to dig up the next city-state, unearthing mosaics and spears, and then shipping them off to a museum. This process of digging down level by level through the various civilizations can take many years as they make their way down to the Stone Age.

Father Thomas Keating, in his book *Intimacy with God: An Introduction to Centering Prayer*, describes the Holy Spirit as a "divine archaeologist."[10] The Spirit starts where we are now, whatever our age, and begins the work of restoration by revealing and healing the most destructive aspects of our addictive behaviors and current relationships. The Spirit then moves deeper and deeper into our lives, not necessarily chronologically, uncovering the bedrock of our earliest emotional life: where we first experienced rejection, trauma, insecurity, or fear. Though this excavation process can be painful, when we offer our hurts to God, we experience cleansing, healing, and greater wholeness. Our relationship with God and other people becomes less cluttered by obstructions.

Maia is a young woman from our community who was recently baptized in the ocean. Just before she was immersed in the chilly waters of the Pacific, she shared how she had been raised in a home filled with brokenness and pain—verbal and emotional abuse as well as physical violence. Her parents separated and got back together numerous times. The family moved sixteen times, which meant sixteen different schools for Maia.

Maia had tried to numb her pain by spending reckless amounts of money. Some days she spent fifty dollars at Starbucks alone! She also tried astrology, numerology, and Buddhism, but nothing brought her the peace she was seeking. Then one day, she opened a Bible she had been given at school but that had been collecting dust in her bedroom. As she began to read, she sensed the whisper of heaven:

"Do not be afraid, look to Jesus and he will carry you through all things."

Overcome with a feeling of peace, love, and safety, she became aware that her sins separated her from Jesus, and so she repented and gave her life to him. Reflecting on her journey, Maia shared, "The strongholds of feeling stupid and worthless, [of] fear and guilt, shame and confusion, depression and loss in my life are melting away by powerful encounters with Jesus' love [which are] transforming me into his unique creation." Now, as Maia sits silently in God's presence, she senses God affirming her and healing the wounds she experienced during childhood.*

Augustine once prayed, "Ancient Beauty, ever new, you were within me, but I was living outside of myself."[11] We experience so much external pressure trying to get our Striving Adam to produce that we can easily begin living outside of ourselves and neglect our Soulful Adam. But when we attend silently to God's presence, the Holy Spirit awakens us to the Ancient Beauty, ever new, that is within us all.

And as we become more aware of the beauty of God's presence in our lives, we experience greater wholeness, or *shalom* (peace).

---

* Along with meditation, God can also use a wise counselor or spiritual director to foster healing in us.

The Music of Heaven

Some years ago, a professor from Wheaton College near Chicago shared with me that he and his wife had wanted to try the grass-fed, hormone-free steaks sold at an upscale butcher shop in their neighborhood, but they felt that the higher cost was far beyond their meager grocery budget. When the professor's wife was pregnant, she had a strong craving to eat good meat, so he went to the butcher and splurged on a steak. As they were eating it for dinner that night, they looked at each other and in unison said, "We can never go back."

In times of stress, rather than turning to the TV, binge drinking, running frantically on the treadmill of work, or using some other addictive habit to numb our pain, we need only to "taste and see that the LORD is good" (Psalm 34:8), and we will find our soul satisfied "in the richest of fare" (Isaiah 55:2).

In Greek mythology, the Sirens were gorgeous, dangerous, half-bird, half-human creatures that lived on rocky islands. Ancient art depicts some of them as mermaids: fish from the waist down and strikingly beautiful women from the waist up. The Sirens sang mesmerizingly beautiful songs that would lure passing sailors to fling themselves over the sides of their ships and swim toward the enchanting voices. But the ships would be destroyed on the jagged rocks surrounding the islands, and the sailors would be eaten by enormous jellyfish. When the Greek hero Odysseus was preparing to sail past the islands of the Sirens, he wanted to hear the Sirens sing. He had his crew tie him to the mast of the ship, and instructed them to fill their ears with wax. As the Sirens sang, Odysseus went mad with desire, but he was securely bound, and because his crew was effectively deaf, they sailed safely past.

In another Greek myth, when Jason and the Argonauts set out on their voyage to pass the isle of the Sirens, they took along Orpheus, the supremely gifted musician. The legend tells us that when Orpheus played his harp, the sublime music made the rocks dance. As Jason and the Argonauts approached the perilous isle, Orpheus played heavenly music on his harp, and the Sirens began to sing. Yet Orpheus' music was even more beautiful than the Sirens' song, and so Jason and his crew sailed past unscathed.

When we wait in stillness in the presence of God, we may find that layers of anger, anxiety, fear, and pain drop like scarves from our ears, and we can attend to the mesmerizingly beautiful song of God's love, which upholds the whole world. With this sublime music ringing in our ears, we are less likely to swim with all our might toward the addictive behaviors that bring temporary pleasure, or the deceitful voices that entice our Striving Adam to pursue success at the cost of something far more valuable. We will be able to make safe passage past monstrous, insatiable desires and the jagged rocks of life's inevitable obstacles and difficulties.

For as we are still before the living God, our souls will be made whole, and our hearts will be set free.

Questions *for* Reflection
and Discussion

———◇———

1. What attracts you about spending time with God in silence? What aversions do you have to meditation?
2. Given your temperament, what physical posture might be most suitable as you practice silent prayer?
3. Is there a simple task you do regularly, such as washing the dishes, vacuuming, walking, or running, that could help you cultivate a greater awareness of God's presence?
4. How might silent prayer help anchor you?
5. How might prayerful meditation affect your relationships with others?

Prayer

Lord, search my heart and excavate what you want to heal in me. Help me sense your abiding love that upholds me and the whole world.

—SEE PSALM 139:23–24

Chapter 5

SABBATH

The Rhythm of Resistance

*In our own contemporary context of the rat race of
anxiety, the celebration of Sabbath is an act of both
resistance and alternative. It is resistance because it
is a visible insistence that our lives are not defined by
production and commodity goods.*[1]

–WALTER BRUEGGEMANN

When I first started working for Sony in Tokyo, a colleague
told me that he had just worked three days and nights
in a row without sleep. As someone raised in North America,
I was incredulous that a person could do that. "How is that even
possible?" I asked.

"I took an energy drink," he replied.

In Japan, these caffeine-laden, supplement-loaded energy
drinks are so potent that they have been banned in North
America—think Red Bull *squared*. Whenever colleagues told
me that they had to work three days straight, I pitied them.
But because I was living in Tokyo, where production is highly

prized and extraordinary sacrifice for the company is valorized, I also admired them.

How can corporations command such allegiance and dedication from their workers? In previous generations, people were accorded status based on their ability to throw a spear into the side of a wild boar and literally bring home the bacon, or to defend their clan against the attacks of barbarians, or because they had inherited a massive estate and an aristocratic title. Today, people are conferred status for advancing in their marketplace careers, excelling in the world of sports or entertainment, or amassing vast wealth and property. Consciously or unconsciously, many people are driven to climb a career ladder not only to enjoy financial security but also to secure a sense of purpose and feel good about themselves.

Sabbath as Resistance: Putting God First

According to Scripture, anything we turn to for our primary source of meaning and validation apart from God is an idol. In the ancient world, idols were literal statues—made of gold, silver, bronze, stone, or wood—before which people bowed down. In the modern world, our idols may not be as concrete or as easily identified, but they are even *more* powerful. And one of the most commonly worshiped idols today is work. The god of work is a hard taskmaster, refusing to let us stop or slow down, running us ragged with little return benefit.

Yet God has long had an alternative, a means of setting us free from the god of work. Exodus 20 instructs us:

Remember the Sabbath day by keeping it holy. Six days
you shall labor and do all your work, but the seventh day
is a Sabbath to the LORD your God. On it you shall not
do any work, neither you, nor your son or daughter, nor
your male or female servant, nor your animals, nor any
foreigner residing in your towns. For in six days the LORD
made the heavens and the earth, the sea, and all that is
in them, but He rested on the seventh day. Therefore,
the LORD blessed the Sabbath day and made it holy
(vv. 8–11).

This fourth commandment, the Sabbath decree, follows
the commandments to put God first, before any other idols,
and to revere his name. It is the only commandment where
the word "holy" is used explicitly.[2] One of the most powerful
antidotes for our tendency to make an idol of our work and
productivity is to honor the Sabbath by setting it apart as a
holy day of rest.

This may sound simple enough, but when was the last time
you took twenty-four hours away from work or anything related
to work? When was the last time you unplugged yourself from
your laptop, email, social media, or smart phone for a day? We
often feel we can't stop working because we are so busy, and
we are afraid of falling behind. Almost everyone I meet says,
"I'm really busy" or, "My life is crazy." Certain stages in life will
invariably be very full and may feel overwhelming. If you are a
parent with young children, or a medical school resident, your
life will probably not feel "balanced." But many of us are busier
than we actually *need* to be, and this is because we feel a *need*
to be "successful." If we are driven by the need to distinguish

ourselves by what we do, we will find ourselves doing many, many things, not all of which are truly necessary. If we are driven by the need to be popular, we will feel compelled to make lots of connections, either in person or online.

Even in our competitive economy, it is possible to trust God by honoring the Sabbath and still succeed financially. The owner of the American restaurant chain Chick-fil-A is a follower of Christ and keeps all their restaurants closed on Sundays. Though most restaurants rely heavily on Sunday sales, the Chick-fil-A chain is still quite profitable.

B&H Photo in Manhattan is the largest non-chain photo and video equipment store in the United States and the second largest in the world. It's also owned and staffed by Hasidic Jews. On any given day, eight to nine thousand people pass through the front door. Seventy percent of their business is online, serviced by a two hundred thousand square-foot warehouse in Brooklyn. Yet even though this industry is intensely competitive, B&H does not conduct business on the Sabbath. They close their doors at 1 p.m. on Fridays and keep them closed all day Saturday, the biggest shopping day of the week. During the Sabbath, customers can peruse the B&H website, but they can't make an online order. Recently, a customer asked the B&H director of communications how they could close both the retail store and the website on Black Friday, the day after Thanksgiving and the busiest shopping day of the year. The director replied, "We respond to a higher authority."[3]

The owners of Chick-fil-A and B&H seek to honor and trust God as they keep the Sabbath. Their business practices are countercultural. In the same way, when we honor the Sabbath commandment, we are taking a stance against mainstream culture. Through our actions, we proclaim, "We answer to a higher authority."

Sabbath as Transformation: Receiving a New Identity

The Sabbath gift was first given to our spiritual forbearers thirty-five hundred years ago. The ancient Israelites had been slaves of the Pharaohs in Egypt for four hundred years—which, biblically speaking, is ten generations. Under the leadership of Moses, they were set free, and on Mount Sinai, God gave them the Ten Commandments, which included the Sabbath decree.

Historian Thomas Cahill tells us that until this point in history, no civilization had ever given ordinary, working people a regular day off.[4] The gift of Sabbath was truly a unique and unprecedented gift, reminding the ancient Hebrews that they were no longer slaves of Pharaoh. Nor were their lives any longer defined by making bricks. The gift of Sabbath forms a new identity within us as well, reminding us that we are not slaves either. Our lives are not defined by our ability to produce or succeed. Our value has *already* been established by the fact that we are beloved by our Maker. We have infinite worth not because of what we do but simply because we are God's sons and daughters.

In the introduction to this book, I described how my friend Jeff told me, "For a long time, you have felt like you needed to be *the guy*." As I resonated with the truth of his words, he added, "I sense God saying: 'You don't need to be *the guy*. You just need to be *the son*.'" I was caught off-guard by his words. I felt an enormous burden lift off my shoulders, and tears came to my eyes—even though we Japanese are not supposed to show emotion in public.

Do you ever feel that you need to be *the guy* or *the girl*?

God has a different word for you.

He says, "You just need to be *my son*." "You just need to be *my daughter*."

We have a three-year-old golden retriever that still acts like a puppy. She's not much of a guard dog. If you were to break into our home, she would probably wag her tail and play with you, or roll over on her back, inviting you to rub her belly. But we don't love our dog because of her production value. We love her simply because she exists.

Our seven-year-old son, Joey, is not particularly productive. He loves to play with his Legos and doesn't enjoy cleaning up. He doesn't earn any money. Yet we love him simply because he exists, because he is breathing. We would lay down our lives for him.

When we remember that we are loved by our Maker before we *do* anything, simply because we *exist*, because we are *breathing*, we are liberated from our enslavement to the god of work. We don't need to try "to stamp existence upon the ghost of our existence."[5] By honoring the Sabbath, we refuse to bow down to the idols of success and productivity. As we embrace the gift of Sabbath, we remember that we are human *beings*, beloved sons and daughters, rather than human *doings*, slaves of a harsh task master. As we live into our identity as beloved children of a liberating God, we will learn to accept our limitations, both our strengths and weaknesses.

Sabbath as Gift:
Beginning from a Place of Rest

After I wrote my first book, an enthusiastic and well-meaning friend said, "Congratulations! You deserve your Sabbath." She meant well, but she was wrong. We don't *deserve* our Sabbath. We don't earn it. We simply receive it as a gift.

According to the Genesis poem, God rested on the seventh day. Adam, the first human being, was made on the sixth day. This means that our first full day on the planet as the human race was a day off. We *began* our existence on the Sabbath. God created us to rest *before* we work. If we violate this order, we damage ourselves and deprive those we love.

> *God created us to rest before we work. If we violate this order, we damage ourselves and deprive those we love.*

We begin our *personal* existence on the Sabbath as well. When we were being formed in the uterus, no matter how ambitious our parents may have been for us, we were not reviewing Mandarin or French flashcards. We were not practicing piano scales in the womb. We were simply in a state of rest.

We also *begin* our day in rest. Most of us view our day as starting in the morning when we wake up, or perhaps after we've had a shower or a cup of coffee. But from a Hebrew perspective, our day begins at sunset in the evening. From the Hebrew point of view, we begin our day at rest. In the creation poem in Genesis 1, we read that there was evening and morning—the first day. There was evening and morning—the second day. This is why the Jewish people begin their Sabbath on Friday evening at sunset. It's a formative practice, reminding us that we begin our days at rest, and while we are resting, God is at work.

If you had stayed over at our house last night, this morning you would have seen the dew on our lawn, the spider webs on the wooden fence in our backyard, the baby figs hanging from our tree, and the cherries blushing orange-pink. God is at work all around us while we sleep. God is also at work in and through us as we sleep. When we face an intractable puzzle, sometimes we just need to go to sleep, and when we wake up, our problem will be solved. As neuroscientists confirm, our mind remains active while we are sleeping, and a night of sleep more than doubles the likelihood that we'll solve a problem requiring insight.[6]

In Scripture, God bestows great gifts on people while they are sleeping. Adam was given his life partner Eve while he was sleeping. Solomon received his legendary gift of wisdom while asleep. Joseph, the adoptive-father of Jesus, heard his most important message from God while he was sleeping. Because God never sleeps, we can. Because God is always at work, we can rest. As Psalm 127 reminds us, it is vain to rise early and sit up late, eating the bread of sorrow, for God "grants sleep to those he loves" (v. 2). The fruit of our work is dependent on God.

In the fourth commandment, we are not only commanded to rest—which, for those of us who are workaholics, is the more relevant one—but we are also commanded to work. When we work, whether with our heads or our hands, we engage in a noble activity and reflect the image of a God who also works. But we *began* our existence at rest. We begin our days at rest. We are called to begin our weeks at rest by receiving the gift of the Sabbath. When we honor this invitation, we work *from a place of rest, rather than desperately needing to rest from our work.*

Sabbath as Grace:
Beginning from a Place of Trust

While pursuing graduate studies, I began to practice a twenty-four-hour Sabbath. Because I regularly had a major exam on Monday morning, I kept my Sabbath from dinnertime on Saturday evening until dinnertime on Sunday evening so that I could study on Sunday night for a Monday morning exam. I wanted to do well academically, and sometimes I felt tempted to crack open the books on my Sabbath to prepare for a test or write a paper, but I felt God inviting me to trust *him* rather than my own capacity.

I am no longer a full-time student, but God continues to invite me to trust him rather than my capacity by honoring the Sabbath. Last year, I was invited to speak to a large national assembly of Pentecostal pastors. I am not a detail-oriented person, and I hadn't read the letter of invitation very carefully. I was under the impression that I was slated to give just one keynote address. A few days before the conference, I noticed that I was slated to give two talks, one of which would require me to prepare a brand-new presentation. As I thought about my schedule, I realized that the only day I could do the necessary preparations would be on my Sabbath, but I felt an invitation to trust God and keep the day of rest. I heeded the call and didn't work on my Sabbath. If you are a Pentecostal minister, you may wonder why that's even a problem. All I needed to do was stand up and let the Holy Spirit fall on me and thunder out an oracle. But I have to confess, I'm not *that* anointed—I actually need to prepare my sermons! So I rested on my Sabbath and discovered that I still had enough time to prepare an extemporaneous talk. Through the gift of Sabbath, I have been learning to live by the "grace of manna" that falls all around me, even when I am tempted to work seven days a week.

Melanie, a member of our faith community, recently completed her last year of medical residency. This final phase of her training involved a demanding clinical work schedule as well as a tough medical board exam. Even though she thought she would need to prepare and study every day, she sensed God inviting her to take a twenty-four-hour period each week to rest and enjoy life, with no studying, computer, or emails. Melanie shares:

> I felt like God was asking me to trust that he would help me pass [the board exam] by his strength, not my own. The other emergency residents and staff doctors discouraged me from taking a Sabbath, which stressed me out at first, especially when I felt they knew the material better. But my husband, family, and church community encouraged me and served me by helping with chores, and God gave me the capacity to get through the weekly material in six days instead of seven. I discovered that I even had "excess time" to run and exercise regularly and to take a weekly class on prayer.

After passing her exam, Melanie expressed her thanks to God in her graduation speech: "I passed the exam and got through residency because of God's love and grace, not by my own strength." That's not to say that if we keep the Sabbath we will always pass our exams or everything we do will be successful. God is calling us to trust him enough to honor the Sabbath and leave the results in his hands.

A respected Christian leader I know was teaching a group of young professionals in New York City. He presented the practice of Sabbath as a kind of circuit breaker on our self-centered ambition: every week we stop whatever we're doing that gives us a sense of worth and significance. Afterward, a young woman approached him. From her face and the tilt of her neck, he could see that she was frustrated and tense. "I am a junior partner, on the partner track at one of the top law firms in this city," she told him. "I know I'm called to this work, and I cannot take a day off. It's impossible with my workload." This leader said to her, "Well, that's the storyline you're telling yourself, but do you know that that narrative is true?"

The young lawyer was very angry and walked away.

Several minutes later, another young woman approached the leader and said that she worked in the same firm as the young woman who had just walked away. This young lawyer told him that she had decided to take a weekly Sabbath. "Part of what makes it possible is I just feel like it's grace—total grace, my success is grace—it just feels like a gift every day. So, if I'm given this gift, why not rest as well." Even though there wasn't a huge difference between these two people in their raw talent or ability, they had a very different way of viewing their narratives. The first young woman's storyline was, "I've *got to strain and seize* this." The other person's narrative was, "This is *pure gift.*"

After reading that story, I know that some of you are thinking, *Ah but with my workload, taking a twenty-four-hour Sabbath is unrealistic!* When we know we're called to our work, we often feel it's impossible to take a day off. But the Sabbath decree reminds us that *this* storyline of striving is not written by God, but one we're telling ourselves. If we make partner, tenure, get the medical residency we want, or achieve our career goals through idolatry, we will be perpetually enslaved to the god of work, which will make us bitter. Though we may keep busy and get a lot of work done, we won't bear lasting fruit. But when we keep the Sabbath holy, we trust God to align our priorities and give us the grace and strength to work hard and tend to what is necessary for six days. We then rest for one, receiving everything as gift.

Can Striving Adam and Soulful Adam really exist in harmony? The fact that the Sabbath commandment calls us to work *and* rest shows us that Striving Adam's drive to work and Soulful Adam's desire to rest can dwell together in unity.

Cultivating Holy Rest

As my colleague Catherine drove to work one very cold February morning, her car hit black ice on the freeway, began spinning, and crashed into a concrete pole. Just before impact, Catherine thought she might die. Her life was spared, but she sustained a serious concussion. Her doctor told her that in order for her brain to heal, she needed to experience REM sleep, the sleep associated with dreaming.

For our souls to experience genuine healing and restoration, we need this imaginative REM-rest as well. Often, when we try really hard to relax—say, we're lying beside a pool on vacation—after seven or eight minutes we start thinking about all the things we ought to be doing, and we begin to feel lazy and unproductive. In order to receive Sabbath as a grace, we must first trust that our world and our lives are being carried along by our Father in heaven. This trust comes to us as we pray and worship God, acknowledging that *God* is God, and *we* are not. As Eugene Peterson summarizes, we make the Sabbath holy when we set aside a day to *pray* and *play*.[7]

Anything that makes us come fully alive *is* a spiritual practice.

When I am doing something physical outdoors, whether running with our dog through the wooded trails near the University of British Columbia, or kayaking or sailing on the ocean, or swimming off the beach, I feel especially alive. You may feel most alive when listening to music, viewing beautiful art, seeing an inspiring film, eating your favorite foods, or spending time with someone very special in your life. As my friend Mark Buchanan says in his book *The Rest of God*, Sabbath is a day to "cease from what is necessary and embrace what gives life . . . to lay hold of whatever you've put off, and pushed away through lack of time, lack of room, lack of breath; it is a day to shuck the *have-to*'s, and lay hold of the *get-to*'s."[8]

Sabbath may sound like an easy practice, but Hebrews tells us that it takes work! The writer of Hebrews encourages us to "Make every effort to enter into that rest" (4:11). Entering Sabbath rest requires effort. As C. S. Lewis observes, busyness for most of us is a form of sloth because we haven't planned well enough in order to embrace rest.[9] Practically, in order to enter into Sabbath, we will need to decide in advance what we *will* do as well as what we *will not* do. On my Sabbath, I take time to sit in quiet meditation with my Maker. I swim. I walk our young son to school. I take our golden retriever through the trails on the edge of our city. I enjoy lunch with my wife, Sakiko, and I regularly barbecue something for dinner, as that doesn't feel like work to me. Engaging in a creative activity *different* from our work on the other five or six days seems like a wise guideline as well. During my Sabbath, I will *not* do any work-related email or social media. I will *not* organize my bills or desk work. I will *not* do any obligatory shopping.

Sabbath may sound like an easy practice, but Hebrews tells us that it takes work!

If you have two days off per week, then one day can be used to run errands and the other can be set aside as a Sabbath. It is important that our Sabbath practices don't become legalistic. In the tradition of Ignatius of Loyola's Prayer of Examen, we can look inside ourselves and ask, "Does this particular activity bring me joy?" Paying attention to what gives us joy or desolation can guide us as to how to honor the Sabbath. Though I am not a particularly gifted gardener, I actually enjoy cutting the grass. But if on my Sabbath, I cut the grass and then say to myself, "Now that I'm on a roll I will also trim the hedge and prune our cherry tree," then it feels like I have crossed the line and am beginning to work. Reading a novel can be a very uplifting experience for me, but if I start thinking seriously about how a particular scene might help me write a sermon or an article, then reading will start to feel like work. I personally love playing and watching sports, but if we are sports fans, we do well to ask if watching a basketball, football, or hockey game is truly relaxing and restorative. Watching a game may entertain us, but it may also leave us emotionally depleted.

Psychologists tell us that our brains tend to miscalculate what will actually bring us happiness. We may think that watching TV is relaxing, but according to a study done by the American Psychological Association, watching more than two hours of television actually leads to feelings of depression. Though walking or hiking may tire us physically, those activities tend to elevate our mood.[10] As we make every effort to honor the Sabbath and keep it holy, we can experiment with practices that bring us joy and draw us close to God.

Cultivating the Desire for Rest

As we embrace any new practice, it will take time to adjust to our new reality. Chemicals in our brain make us crave the adrenaline rush of constant, intense work like an alcoholic craves a drink. Checking email or social media on our smart phone can also become addictive, because when we open up a new message, it literally lights up the pleasure center in our brain as we get a dollop of reward hormones.[11] In fact, if you are not used to taking any time away from work, the practice of keeping Sabbath rest may feel stressful at first.

The president of a theological graduate school shared with me an experience he had taking time away from the day-to-day grind of his job. After leading his school through a major capital campaign, he and his wife traveled to Wales so they could step off the hamster wheel of achievement and relax. They stopped using a cell phone, the internet, and email. As they walked, read, slept, ate, and talked, they moved from a lifestyle characterized by doing and performing into one marked by silence, contemplation, and being.

But something unexpected happened while he was in

Wales. "I experienced significant withdrawal pains, both psychologically and physically," he confessed. "I yearned for work and production and was troubled by having nothing to do. For me it was a significant crisis." By exclusively pursuing work, he had valued doing more than being. Sabbath had been squeezed out of his life. After returning home, he resolved to live a new rhythm marked by a diligent observance of Sabbath. He kept a twenty-four-hour day of rest when there would be no email, internet, or computer use of any kind. He spent time worshiping in community, with family or friends, or in the garden, but he did nothing remotely related to work. After honoring a weekly Sabbath for nearly a year, he was surprised by how the regular practice of Sabbath produced an unexpected outcome—"the deepening sense of *shalom* [peace]."[12]

The habit of honoring the Sabbath not only energizes our work but also makes our workweek more prayerful and fruitful. As we explored in the previous chapter, when we engage in a simple rhythm of morning prayer, we become more mindful of God throughout the day. Saint Benedict teaches that if we have a regular rhythm of prayer (even if it is brief), then our work itself can become prayer. His teaching is summarized in the expression: "To pray is to work" and "to work is to pray."

Through the gift of Sabbath, we remember that we don't need to live by the sweat of our brow alone but by the grace of manna falling all around us. Through this grace, we realize we don't need to be *the guy* or *the girl* because we are already *the son* or *the daughter*. The gift of this sacred day teaches us that we don't need to stamp existence on the ghost of our existence. As your Striving Adam drives you to succeed, do you also hear God calling you to embrace your Soulful Adam by trusting him enough to embrace the gift of Sabbath? This is an invitation you cannot afford to refuse.

Jesus says, "Get away with me, and you will recover your life. I won't put anything ill-fitting on you, but I will teach you the unforced rhythms of grace; I will teach you how to live light and free, in body and in soul."[13]

Questions *for* Reflection
and Discussion

———◆———

1. Do you currently have a twenty-four-hour period when you completely rest from work (including work-related emails, texts, and social media)?
2. Do you have any fears (or challenges) around living with a twenty-four-hour Sabbath?
3. In what ways might keeping the Sabbath shape your identity as a child of God?
4. How would honoring the Sabbath deepen your trust in God?
5. How might you plan ahead so that you can embrace Sabbath rest?
6. Given your unique character, what would bring you the most life on your Sabbath? What would end up draining you?

Prayer

God of rest, I'm so busy. The demands of life are piled high, and my schedule is a tyrant. Help me catch my breath and enter the gift of your Sabbath once more. Free me to enjoy the goodness of your favor and this life. Forgive me for all the ways I try to justify myself by my accomplishments. Help me to rest every day in your grace. Amen.[14]

Chapter 6

GRATITUDE

Savoring God's Gifts

I don't have to chase extraordinary moments to find
happiness—it's right in front of me if I'm paying
attention and practicing gratitude.

–BRENÉ BROWN

My son, Joey, and I recently read the children's book *Making Heart-Bread* by Matthew, Dennis, and Sheila Linn. The story begins with Rachel, a young girl who is learning from her grandmother how to make bread.

As they make bread together, the grandmother tells Rachel about "tummy bread," which fills our tummies, and "heart bread," which fills our hearts. The grandmother tells Rachel that when she was a little girl, she lived in Europe during the war. Like a lot of other children, she lost her parents and her home and became very hungry. Eventually, she was given shelter in a refugee home, and the adults there were loving and kind. But she and the other children had trouble sleeping at night, because they remembered that they had been homeless and hungry, and they feared that one day they might not be able to eat again.

One of the wise adults decided to give each of the children a piece of bread to hold at bedtime. With this bread in their hands, the children remembered, "I ate today, and I will eat again tomorrow." Holding onto this bread, all of them slept in peace.

This story, based on actual events, is one of the best visual explanations I've ever come across for the Prayer of Examen, a thanksgiving ritual created by the sixteenth-century Spanish priest Ignatius of Loyola. This is a prayer that has been practiced by followers of Jesus all over the world for the past five centuries. At the end (or beginning) of each day, the examen instructs us to review the previous twenty-four hours of our lives and think about what we have experienced: our meetings and conversations, our projects and the tasks, how we've used any discretionary time. As we think about the events of our day and the thoughts and the feelings that accompanied us, we ask ourselves several questions. *Where did I feel most alive? Where did I feel the most joy? When did I feel most connected to my Creator?* Then we give thanks to God for these things.

In reviewing our day, we also ask: *Where did I feel most anxious, frustrated, or angry? When did I feel most disconnected from myself and my Creator?* Then we lift these things up to God in prayer and become free of them. Recounting how God has fed our bodies and our hearts is like holding bread in our hands. We look at what God has done, and we say, "I was fed today. God will feed me tomorrow." When we feel loved, we feel more gratitude and joy, and we also sleep better.

Let me give an example of my examen from this past Monday (I set an alarm on my watch to remind me to pray the examen each evening). I was grateful to be able to swim that morning. I have a bad ankle from an old sports injury in high school, so I can't run very far, but I can still swim, and I am thankful for that. Monday is my day off, and so I take Joey, our second grader, to school. Whenever I take him to school, we're often running behind schedule. While I walked our golden retriever, Sasha, on her harness leash, Joey rode his scooter. Then Joey had an idea. He said, "This is my sleigh, and Sasha is my reindeer!" Sasha is as strong as a husky, so we latched her leash onto the handlebars and took off running. We were having a great time—and thankful that my wife wasn't there! Sure enough, Joey wiped out, but thank God he didn't hurt himself, because then *I* would have been in big trouble! I was thankful for that as well.

I was also grateful for a delicious curry dinner we enjoyed that night.

Take a few minutes now to think about the last twenty-four hours. Reflect on something that you are thankful for, something that made you feel alive and gave you joy.

Now say "thank you" to God. You have just prayed the examen.

Thanksgiving as a Habit

As we cultivate this practice of regularly giving thanks each day, we will carry it forward into the rest of our lives as well. Whenever we experience something good, we'll begin to say to ourselves, "This is something I can use for my examen tonight." But we'll also savor joy in the moment. When we become people who give thanks for what has happened in the past, we will also become people who savor the present moment.

David Steindl-Rast, a Benedictine monk, says, "It is not joy that makes us grateful; it is gratitude that makes us joyful."[1] Benedictine monks and nuns memorize all hundred and fifty psalms in the Bible. Then they pray these psalms—many of which are filled with thanksgiving—on a weekly cycle. So Brother David is training himself in the practice of gratitude as he gives thanks over and over and over again each day. Because monks have trained their hearts to be grateful, they experience deep, consistent joy.

Research shows that grateful people experience a 25 percent spike in alertness and energy—and they also sleep better.[2] According to MRI scans that detect when the pleasure center in our brain lights up, monks may well be the happiest people on earth. Who would have guessed that those who take vows of poverty, chastity, and obedience would be the planet's most contented residents? But monks have trained their minds through practices such as meditation to embrace the gift of the present moment.[3]

It is not joy that makes us grateful; it is gratitude that makes us joyful.

Of course, the habit of thanksgiving is not only a practice for monks and nuns.

Author Ann Voskamp knows the transforming power of giving thanks. She is no stranger to heartbreak. As a four-year-old girl, her younger sister had toddled into the farm lane, wandering after a cat. Not seeing her there, a delivery truck driver accidently drove over her, crushing her to death. Ann also lost her two infant nephews (within a year-and-a-half window) to a rare genetic lung disease. A farmer's wife and a homeschooling mother of seven (including a recently adopted baby girl from China), Ann's life has plenty of demands. And like the rest of us, she at times feels like a failure, a loser, not enough.

Several years ago, a friend of Ann's dared her to name one thousand gifts in her life.* So began her practice of giving thanks—even for the smallest things:

1. *Morning shadows across old floors*
2. *Jam piled high on the toast*
3. *Cry of the blue jay from high in the spruce . . .*

"You've changed," another friend remarked. Ann had grown visibly more hopeful. Grateful. Happy.

"It's the list, isn't it?" her friend surmised. As thanksgiving grew into a practice, her life was transformed. She became more aware of God's goodness and joy in the ordinary moments of her day.[4]

Most Christians are familiar with Jesus' words from John: "I am the way and the truth and the life" (14:6). Even though we often see Jesus as the *truth*—the embodiment of all wisdom—and we also see Jesus as the *life*—both in the world to come and

---

* This subsequently became the basis of the beloved *New York Times* bestseller *One Thousand Gifts*.

as the fullness of God's life now—we often fail to see Jesus as the *way* we are called to live our lives here and now. Yet when the invisible, infinite God parted the curtain between heaven and earth, he stepped onto our planet as a human being and lived a perfect life among us in Jesus. And the *way* Jesus lived is a perfect model for how we are called to live today. Jesus took time to savor the good gifts of life and to give thanks. Ann Voskamp recognizes this—and she does the same.

The devout Hebrews of Jesus' day also believed that our hearts could be trained in gratitude, and so they had a practice called "the eighteen benedictions a day." *Bene* is the root word for "good," and *diction* is the term for "word." When devout Jews got up in the morning, they would thank God for eighteen things. At noon, they would thank God for eighteen things. In the evening, they would thank God for eighteen things. They did this because they believed that our hearts could be nurtured in gratitude.

Giving thanks for eighteen things three times a day may sound overwhelming. Shawn Achor, a psychologist who teaches at Harvard, suggests that we can train our brains to become more grateful by setting aside just *five minutes* a day for practicing gratitude. He cites a one-week study in which people were asked to take five minutes a day, at the same time every day, to write down three things they were thankful for. They didn't have to be big things, but they had to be concrete and specific, such as, "I'm thankful for the delicious Thai take-out dinner I had last night." Or, "I'm thankful that my daughter gave me a hug." Or, "I'm thankful that my boss complimented my work." The participants simply expressed thanks for three specific things at the same time every day.

At the end of one month, the researchers followed up and found that those who practiced gratitude—including those who *stopped* the exercise after one week—were happier and less depressed. Remarkably, after three months, the participants who had been part of the one-week experiment were still more joyful and content. Incredibly, after the six-month mark, they were still happier, less anxious, and less depressed.

> *We can train our brains to become more grateful by setting aside just* **five minutes** *a day for practicing gratitude.*

The researchers hypothesized that the simple practice of writing down three thanksgivings a day over the course of a week primed the participants' minds to search for the good in their lives.[5]

Let's say you are in the market for a white Honda Civic. You're thinking about buying one, but you aren't sure. Then you begin to notice white Honda Civics everywhere. It's not as if the people at the Honda dealership have conspired to push you over the edge by flooding your neighborhood and the area around your workplace with white Honda Civics. Rather, because your mind is primed to think about them, you begin to notice them more. When we practice giving thanks on a regular basis, it is not as if more good things are coming into our lives. Rather, our minds are primed to notice good things, and so we become more grateful, joyful, and content—even though nothing around us has actually changed. But when it comes to cultivating a heart of gratitude, it's important to make this habit of thanksgiving a ritual, ideally at the same time every day.

Mason Currey, the author of *Daily Rituals: How Artists Think*, observes that the greatest artists often have very precise rituals for their work.[6] Though we may tend to think of artists as spontaneous, random, and unstructured in their work habits, Currey's book reveals that 161 of the world's leading artists, writers, musical composers, and filmmakers have ingrained, habitual practices. For example, the writer Anne Lamott sits down to write every day (except her Sabbath) at 9:00 a.m. As soon as her bum hits the chair, her subconscious says, "Annie, it is time to be creative!"[7] Tom Wolfe, the famous novelist, begins to write each night at midnight. When the clock strikes midnight, his subconscious says, "It's time to be creative!" Through a daily ritual, we can train our minds to be more creative at certain times. In the same way, a thanksgiving ritual can train our spirits to be more *grateful* in all circumstances.[8]

Thanksgiving as a Portal into the Presence of God

Even if you already think of yourself as a grateful person, we all need to be reminded again and again to give thanks—and to continue to cultivate a heart of thanksgiving. We see this invitation to give thanks repeated throughout the Bible. For instance:

- The psalmist says: "Enter his gates with thanksgiving and his courts with praise" (Psalm 100:4).
- David says, "Praise the LORD, my soul, and forget not all his benefits" (Psalm 103:2).
- The apostle Paul says, "Give thanks in all circumstances; for this is God's will for you" (1 Thessalonians 5:18).

- Jesus gives thanks to his Father in heaven before breaking the bread to feed the multitudes (Mark 6:41; 8:6).

Part of what it means to walk in the *way* of Jesus is to savor the good gifts that we receive and to give thanks to God for those gifts. As we do this, we nurture a heart of gratitude and humility. If you're in the mood for an experiment, take a twenty-four-hour period, and every time you meet people, criticize them or complain about something. You will notice that people will begin to feel alienated from you, and they may even lean away from you as you criticize them, whine, or complain.

Then pick another twenty-four-hour period, and whenever you meet people, thank them or compliment them. At the coffee shop, you might say to the barista, "That is an amazing white leaf you created!" You'll notice that people are leaning toward you, maybe even literally, as they savor your words of appreciation and affirmation.

So it is when we give thanks to God. We will find God's presence feels nearer to us.[9] Even though God is everywhere, the Bible tells us that God mysteriously *inhabits* the praises of his people (Psalm 22:3). When we thank and praise God, his presence inhabits our lives more and more. We might think of thanksgiving as a portal to the presence of God.

To be clear, it is okay to complain to God (Psalm 13), even to scream and shake your fist like Job. God can handle our emotional honesty. But if the *only* way we communicate with God is by complaining, cursing, or whining, we will feel alienated from God. Conversely, when we take time to thank God and affirm his goodness, we will draw closer to him. And as we draw closer to God, enjoying his presence and the gift of his friendship, we will be transformed.

Cultivating Joyful Humility

Gratitude also slays the foe of comparison. As a friend of mine says, "Envy is the thief of joy." Even those who have far more money, talent, or resources than others are not necessarily grateful—because they're often too busy comparing themselves with people who have even more. We all probably know busy, achievement-oriented people who seem to think that because of their education, success at work, or grandiose accomplishments, they are better than the rest of us and therefore are entitled to better treatment. This attitude not only makes them tedious to be with, but it also makes them joyless, because their expectations about how they feel they deserve to be treated usually exceed their actual experiences.

My friend Pete Scazzero, a pastor and author, asked his literary agent if there was any danger in becoming a successful author. "That's easy," she answered, "I can sum it up in one word: entitlement. Some authors have a lot of influence after they become well known. They change. They walk into a room acting as if everyone in the world revolves around them. They become miserable to work with."

Now, if anyone in the history of our planet could have had a sense of entitlement, it would have been Jesus. As it says in the book of Revelation, Jesus is the King of kings and the Lord of lords (19:16). If ever there was royalty, if ever there was a VIP, it was Jesus. Yet he never acted as if the world revolved around him or assumed that he was entitled to special treatment. Jesus said, "[I] did not come to *be* served, but to serve and to give [my] life as a ransom for all" (Mark 10:45, italics mine).

Even though Jesus is the unique Son of God and has a special and intimate relationship with his Father, he prays, "Father, I thank you that you have heard me" (John 11:41). And even though he was involved in the creation of our planet before he came into the world as a human being, when he receives loaves of bread and fish from a young boy, he doesn't say, "Hey, these already belong to me." Rather, he gives thanks to God for them (John 6:8–11).

Jesus did not have a sense of entitlement, and he overflowed with gratitude.

Entitlement kills gratitude. Let's say you want to buy a car, and so you work hard, save money, go to the dealership, and buy a Ford. As you drive your car off the dealer's lot, chances are that you are not feeling an immense sense of gratitude toward the dealer—unless he gave you an amazing deal. Nor are you feeling thankful for the people who assembled the car, nor to Henry Ford, because it was *you* who *worked* for it, saved your money, and bought it. But let's say that a mere acquaintance comes up to you, dangles some keys, and says, "Hey, guess what? I'm giving you a brand-new Ferrari." If this actually happened to you tomorrow, you would probably jump up and down like a contestant on *The Price Is Right!* You might even hug the person, grateful to receive such an incredible gift from a person you hardly know![10] When we are free from a sense of entitlement, we can become truly grateful.

Giving thanks also paves the way for a person to respond to the impulses of Striving Adam and climb a career ladder, yet remain humble in the process. In the Scriptures, we see Daniel rising to a top position in the government of Babylon. As people observed his life, they were struck by his wisdom, courage, and humility. The only way they could explain his extraordinary character was to say, "The spirit of the gods is in you" (Daniel 5:14). How did Daniel become a person of such mysterious beauty? He didn't leave it to chance. When Daniel learned that the king made it a crime punishable by death for anyone who worshiped any god except the king, Daniel risked his life, went home, and prayed. Three times a day he knelt and *gave thanks* as had been his regular practice (Daniel 6:10). As Daniel offered thanks to God, he was able to stave off any sense of entitlement that could have come with his lofty position, and instead he grew in gratitude and humility.

Colman Mockler, the late legendary CEO of Gillette, was another man who occupied a high post and yet embodied humility. Mockler fought off three hostile takeover bids (even though he could have pocketed millions of dollars if he had capitulated) in order to protect the interests of thousands of employees and the shareholders. Under his guidance, sales and the company stock value soared. Those around him were impressed by his integrity, humility, and work-life balance. Even during the most intense times, Mockler did not significantly reduce the amount of time spent with his family, rarely working evenings or weekends. Mockler was able to build a great company *and* become a great person because God was at the core of his life.

Even as his work responsibilities grew as the company became increasingly global, Mockler maintained disciplined worship practices. In addition to prioritizing weekly Sunday worship, each morning he would turn his day over to God, praying: "Lord, I have no idea how to make the decisions I have to make today, but I know you do and I'm going to trust you to show me."[11] Jim Collins, author of the bestselling *Good to Great*, describes Mockler as an exemplary CEO and even compared him to Abraham Lincoln. Both Mockler's and Lincoln's fierce Striving-Adam resolve and humble Soulful-Adam character were shaped by their deep faith and dependence on God.[12]

Yes, it's possible to rise to significant heights with Striving Adam's tenacity all the while maintaining Soulful Adam's spirit of humility and gratitude—if we turn to God and give him thanks.

Savoring Each Sweet Day

In the movie *About Time*, a father and his twentysomething son have the power to time-travel: whenever they close their eyes, clench their fists, and vividly remember something from the past, they go back to that moment and relive it. The dad gives his son, Tim, some advice about how to use this power: "You should live an ordinary life, living it day by day, like anyone else, but *to live every day again* almost exactly the same, the first time with all the tensions and worries that stop you noticing how sweet the world can be. But the second time noticing."

Tim lives a day in which he and his colleague-best friend Rory go through the unpleasant experience of seeing Rory unfairly scolded by their boss at the law firm where they work. Later in the day, Tim buys a sandwich and drink at a convenience store, but is preoccupied with other matters and absent-mindedly receives the food. He rushes through a train station to catch a train, and then wins a case in court. As he rides the subway home, he is annoyed by the loud music emanating from the guy sitting next to him.

The *second* time he lives this day, when Rory is unfairly scolded, Tim furtively writes out a sign that says, "DICK," with an arrow pointed at the boss (and I'm pretty sure his name is not Richard). Then, when Tim buys his sandwich and drink, he makes eye contact with the cashier, smiles, and says, "Thank you." As he runs through the train station, he marvels at the magnificent arched ceiling of the beautiful historic building. Later on, when his client is declared not guilty, he hugs him. On the subway ride home, as he hears the music from the guy sitting next to him, he enjoys the tune and plays along in the air.

By the end of the movie, Tim has an epiphany: "I think I've learned the final lesson from my travels in time; and I have even gone one step further than my father did. The truth is now I don't travel back at all, not even for the day. I just try to live every day as if I've deliberately come back to this one day, to enjoy it as if it was the full final day of my extraordinary, ordinary life."

Jesus invites us to live each day as if it were our full final day, so that the tensions and the stresses of our day don't stop us from savoring its sweet gifts and thanking God for them.

When meeting with a couple whose wedding I will officiate, I often say, "Your wedding day can be so busy and stressful that you can miss the sweetness of it. So make sure that amidst all the little details, you take time to *savor* the gift of this most beautiful day. Otherwise, it will blow past you in a blur." And so it is with all the busyness and the stress of life, which can just blow past us in a blur. Let us take time to savor the sweetness. But we don't need to time-travel to reexamine the story of our lives.

Savoring the Story of Our Lives

On a recent retreat, I took time to write down the most life-shaping events of my life. As I reviewed my list, I noticed that *none* of the major turning points were things that I had orchestrated:

> our family moving from Japan to London when I was
>   a toddler,
> being caught shoplifting as a teenager,
> being invited by a family friend to a Christian summer camp,
> being introduced by a friend to my future wife,
> receiving a sense of direction for my current work.

I also became conscious of the many people who helped me along the way. Because people describe me as a hard-working, proactive, type-A person, it stunned me that the most important doors of my life opened as a gift.

As we reexamine our life stories—the family and country we were born into, the people who influenced us, the opportunities we've had—we will often notice that the most important elements of our lives have been utter gifts. Though we may work very hard and make the most of every opportunity, nearly every step of our journey traces a story of grace.

When we realize that our lives are pure gift, we are less likely to grab at life with a sense of entitlement. We are more likely to find ourselves inspired to work with the diligence of Striving Adam *and* live in the humble awareness of grace with eyes of Soulful Adam. Instead of being filled with nervous energy, we will exude humility and serenity. When we recognize that our lives are being orchestrated by God, we will be free to enjoy the gift of Sabbath more fully, and we will become people of extravagant worship and generous contribution as we joyfully think of ways to thank our Maker.

Though we may work very hard and make the most of every opportunity, nearly every step of our journey traces a story of grace.

If you go to the gym once and lift weights, you are not going to get stronger—you're just going to be sore. If you go for a long run once or twice, you are not going to have more endurance—you're just going to feel tired. But if you keep exercising for a long time, your body will change. And so it is with giving thanks to God. It might not change your life right away, but if you keep giving thanks to God *every* day, *you* will change. You will become more grateful, more content, and more joyful as you become more connected with your *Maker*.

As I write these words, I am aware of the health challenges of my own father, who is on home dialysis, with failing eyes and kidneys. My mom is the primary caregiver, and though she is often exhausted, she is also incredibly grateful to God and appreciative of others. When I contemplate my mom's genuine joy, contentment, and gratitude, I think, "*That* is what a transformed heart looks like. *That* is what it looks like to follow God in the same direction for a really long time." As you make thanksgiving to God a habit, one day your children, nephews, nieces, and others around you will look at you and say, "*That* is what a transformed heart looks like. *That is* what it looks like to follow God in the same direction for a long time."

Questions *for* Reflection
and Discussion

———————◇———————

1. What are you most grateful for right now?
2. How might a daily practice of gratitude help you become more aware of God's goodness?
3. Is there a time each day when you could begin a thanksgiving ritual? If doing this every day feels overwhelming at first, is there a time you could do this once or twice each week?
4. If you were to examine your life thus far, how would you complete the sentence: "My life is the story of _____."
5. How might the prayer of examen shape your character over time?

Prayer

Lord,
You have given so much to me,
Give one thing more — a grateful heart.

                                     –GEORGE HERBERT

Chapter 7

SIMPLE ABUNDANCE

Why Less Is More

Simplicity gives freedom.[1]
–RICHARD FOSTER

When I was twelve years old, I had a passion for motorcycles. I didn't own one, but one of my best friends did, and he allowed me to ride it from time to time. One day, I was at the motorcycle shop with my mother and grandmother, who was visiting from Tokyo. As I was *ooh*-ing and *ahh*-ing over a Suzuki dirt bike, my grandmother said, "Ken, if you like the bike so much, I'll buy it for you." I felt myself floating toward heaven . . . until I heard the voice-over of my mother saying to my grandmother, "You will *not* buy him that motorcycle. If he gets into an accident, you will be responsible for that for the rest of your life." My grandmother began nodding and withdrew her offer. I found myself free-falling from the peak of delight into the pit of despair!

Can material things bring us happiness? Philosophers, social scientists, psychologists, and theologians continue to wrestle with this ancient question. In brain scans of people recalling times of feeling close to God in prayer, worship, or solitude, neurologists have discovered that a certain part of the brain, the *caudate nucleus*, lights up. In brain scans of people viewing pictures of material possessions, such as iPods, Harley-Davidson motorcycles, and red Ferraris, neurologists discovered that the *exact same place* in their brain lights up.[2] Material goods *can* bring us momentary happiness as the chemical dopamine is released in our brain. But research also shows that material things cannot provide *long-term* satisfaction or happiness.

A truly happy, contented life does not require nearly as much money as we may think. Author Malcom Gladwell once asked, "How much money does a family need in order for the parents to be able to raise their children in an ideal way?"[3] Research has revealed that a certain amount of money does, in fact, provide a minimal level of happiness, but after that point, additional income ceases to have any noticeable effect. For example, if your household makes $75,000 per year, but your neighbors make $100,000, they may be able to drive a nicer car than you and go out to eat a little more often, but they won't necessarily be any happier than you or better equipped to do the thousands of small and large things good parenting requires. Gladwell also points out that while extreme poverty makes parenting more difficult, extreme wealth is no picnic, either. "Honey, we can't buy that," from a parent of modest means becomes, "Honey, we *won't* buy that," from a richer parent.

As a pastor who has been exposed to people across the financial spectrum, I have observed that even though poverty can make raising a family more difficult, having a vast amount of money also poses challenges. You may be saying, "I want *that* difficulty!" But children from a very wealthy family may have a greater sense of entitlement and may have a harder time feeling empathy and compassion for others. Ironically, if we pursue happiness through the acquisition of material possessions, we will become chronically discontent and unhappy. But as we pursue a simpler life and grow in our dependence on God— trusting that we are being cared for by him—a deeper and more enduring sense of well-being, peace, and joy will be nurtured within us. While material things, such as nice clothes, a nice car, a nice home, do elicit a certain amount of pleasure, they can only deliver the *lowest* level of happiness. The *highest* levels of happiness come from generativity—offering life to others and surrendering to an unconditional, infinite love.

Following the Path of Jesus

Jesus' life provides an ideal model of what joyful simplicity and dependence on God can deliver.

Scripture tells us that the invisible, infinite God parted the curtain between heaven and earth and stepped into our neighborhood as the flesh-and-blood human being we know as Jesus Christ. Jesus was the only person in history who got to choose his life circumstances *before* he was born.

If you could have determined your financial net worth before coming into the world, where would you have pegged it? Or, if a genie suddenly appeared before you right now and offered to increase your annual income to whatever you wanted, how many zeroes would you add? If you are like me, your knee-jerk reaction might be, "Whatever Bill Gates is making sounds good. Or Mark Zuckerberg. Or Oprah Winfrey. Adjusted for inflation, of course, every year."

Curiously, Jesus—who could have chosen a net worth greater than any person in the history of the world—chose to live very humbly. He was born in a borrowed barn and immediately became a refugee. When Mary and Joseph dedicated him at the temple, they offered two pigeons as a sacrifice, indicating that Jesus was born into a family at the very lowest economic bracket in Israel. Based on Joseph's vocation, we also know that Jesus may well have been a carpenter before he became a rabbi. However, the Greek word usually translated as "carpenter," *tekton*, can also be translated as "day laborer."

When I ride my bike down Ontario Street in our city, I regularly see a group of men standing at a certain corner who look as though they have fallen on financial hard times. They're waiting to be picked up by some construction crew as a day laborer. As I ride past them, I sometimes imagine Jesus among them. When Jesus made the transition from being a blue-collar laborer to a white-collar teacher, he could have leveraged his popularity for financial advantage. But he chose to remain financially poor, and he even chose to be homeless for part of his life (Luke 9:58).

So why would the infinite God, who could have secured his income at any level, choose to live in the world without the net worth of the founder of IKEA, or even at a solid middle-class level? In part, because Jesus wanted to show us that God chooses to stand in solidarity with the poor. According to the World Bank, 71 percent of the world lives on ten dollars or less a day.[4] The Bible teaches that God is especially close to the brokenhearted, the poor, and the disenfranchised (Psalm 34:18). By becoming one of them in the person of Jesus Christ, God is saying, "I stand with the poor." Jesus also chose to be financially poor because he knew that money and material possessions could clutter and even suffocate our relationship with God (Matthew 6:24), making it impossible for us to breathe spiritually and receive the gift of God's love and concern for us.

Moreover, Jesus chose to live with a very modest amount of money because he wanted to learn to depend on God. In a mysterious verse in the book of Hebrews, we see that Jesus Christ learned obedience to God through what he suffered (5:8). Jesus Christ wasn't born into our world as a fully mature human being. Like you and me, he had to learn to eat, walk, talk, read, and write, and to grow in maturity. He also learned over time to depend on God for his daily needs. When Jesus taught us to pray, "Give us this day our daily bread," he was teaching us his own prayer, because he also prayed to God, his Father, for *his* daily bread.

Choosing Simple Abundance

But what does it mean for us to walk in the footsteps of Jesus toward simplicity and deeper dependence on God? As we see in the Gospels, Jesus didn't have a high income, a home of his own, or many of our world's luxuries, conveniences, and comforts (Matthew 8:20). Rather, he experienced much suffering and adversity in his life. And yet, Scripture tells us that he had a joy that surpassed his peers.

This joy came from his ever-deepening relationship with God, whose love he treasured. Because he felt nourished, uplifted by God, and truly content, he didn't pine after material things that he didn't need. When we grow in deeper dependence on God and treasure his love and care, we will discover an abiding joy and contentment that the world around us does not know (John 14:27). We will also find ourselves craving fewer things we don't really need and instead longing to open our hands and share from the fullness that we have been given.

On a recent overnight flight to Manila in the Philippines, I found myself unexpectedly upgraded to business class. I entered the cabin, sat down, and felt very grateful. The flight attendant, Maria, greeted me and gave me a menu. The choices made me feel like I was in a fancy restaurant! Even though I'd already eaten dinner, the beef tenderloin with prawns and papaya salad sounded delicious. I thought, *This is too good to pass up! I may never get upgraded again.* So I ordered one of the entrées.

But then I realized that I wasn't actually hungry, and I didn't want *another* dinner. I caught Maria's eye and told her that even though I'd ordered an entrée, I'd already eaten dinner and wasn't really hungry. So I asked her to cancel my order. My opportunistic side encouraged me to stay up to enjoy the business class service, but with a full schedule facing me in Manila, I chose to sleep instead.

When we feel full, we don't crave foods that we don't need. Though we may be attracted to what a menu offers or by the pastries on display at the bakery, we won't crave food when we're already satisfied. So it is when our hearts feel full because we know that we are already being cared for by a loving God in whom we live and move and have our being. As we experience the wonder of our Father's provision, we will find that we yearn for fewer things we don't need.

I was walking with a woman who is quite wealthy and very generous past some swanky shops in the downtown area of a city when she said to me, "Let me buy you an Armani suit." I remember in that moment feeling curious about what an Armani suit might feel like but also thinking, *I certainly don't need or want one, at least not enough for her to buy me one.* I turned to her and said, "Thank you, but I don't need one."

She then said, "Well, how about a new watch? Rolexes are really good watches."

"So I've heard," I replied, "but I've got a digital, waterproof Timex here, and 'it takes a licking and keeps on ticking!' I know that a Rolex is a great watch, but I'm so absentminded that if you bought me one I would be filled with anxiety over losing it. So, thank you, but no." I really appreciated this person's care for me, but when we are satisfied, we simply don't crave what we don't need.

One of the ways we can follow the path of Christ's dependence on God is to cultivate daily rhythms, such as meditation and practicing gratitude, so that we can experience deep contentment, joy, and confidence in our everyday life with God.[5] One of the practical benefits of this way of life is that we won't feel compelled to work seventy or eighty hours each week to keep up with the "Joneses" or the "Lees." Though we may work very hard, we will be working hard for the right reasons.

Decumulating

Another way we can follow Christ on the path toward simplifying our lives and fostering a greater dependence on God is by decumulating. Scripture tells us that although Jesus Christ was unimaginably rich in heaven, he took on the status of a slave, so that through his poverty, we might become truly rich in the only way that matters (Philippians 2:1–11). By decumulating, we follow Jesus on this path of humility.

Marie Kondo, in her international bestseller *The Life-Changing Magic of Tidying Up: The Japanese Art of Decluttering and Organizing*, advises us to gather together all our clothes and place them in a pile. Then we are to pick up each item and ask, "Does this bring me joy?" If not, suggests Kondo, we should toss it out. We're to do the same with our books, papers, and miscellaneous things, such as sporting goods and knick-knacks. Although Kondo is not a Christian, the exercise is similar to the classic Ignatian prayer of examen that I've mentioned a few times already. In the examen, we ask if something brings us life, joy, and a sense of gratitude to God. If so, we embrace and give thanks for it. Conversely, if we feel something brings frustration, anxiety, depression, and a sense of distance from God, we must let it go. In a countercultural way, Kondo doesn't advise us to decide what to get *rid of*, but rather what we will *keep*. Kondo points out that when we have fewer things, we have a deeper enjoyment of those things. For example, if we have a *large* number of books and a *few* great books, our attention will be diffused. But if we have just a few treasured books, we will enjoy and benefit from them more.

As a pastor who has visited the homes of people from a wide range of backgrounds, I find that people who are anxious about whether they will have enough for tomorrow have a harder time getting rid of things, and their homes tend to be more cluttered. On the other hand, people who are confident about the future tend to have less cluttered living spaces. They are less fearful about whether they will need something in the future, particularly material objects. If we believe in a God who is faithful to provide all that we need, then regardless of our income, we can live with more contentment and confidence as we face the future. And we will also be able to part with our stuff more easily. My friend Mike describes how he and his wife Danae's ongoing experience of purging allows him to declutter:

I start in my closet, pulling out one thing and then another.

"Are you sure?" Danae asks as I pull out another shirt.

"Yup," I say. "I haven't worn that shirt in a year."

Danae picks it up and looks at it. "You're right, you haven't."

"What about this?" I ask, pulling out a suit I got when I was eighteen.

"I've never even *seen* that suit before," Danae says with a laugh. "Where have you been hiding it?"

I add it to the pile.

"And these?" I hold up a pair of nice shoes that haven't been worn in more than a year.

"Gone," says Danae.

All told, I clean out ten shirts, two pairs of jeans, that nice pair of shoes, my pristine suit, and a whole pile of T-shirts that I will never wear. . . .

While I used to consider the accumulation of items in my life an indication of my gradually increasing wealth, they now remind me of the hair and soap scum that accumulates in my bathtub drain until I find myself standing in two inches of tepid water."[6]

Through the process of decumulating and purging, Mike observes, "I feel free."[7] Mike and Danae experience the joy of simplifying their lives. Having released burdensome piles of clutter, they feel lighter and can enjoy greater freedom and spaciousness. As we simplify our lives, we have more space literally and figuratively to experience the rich life of the Spirit. Out of this sense of abundance (Ephesians 3:14–19), we can freely choose a path of generosity. In fact, one of the best ways to honor Striving Adam's passion to achieve and Soulful Adam's desire to serve others is to realize that we are called to produce, not merely to enrich ourselves or prop up our ego, but to bless others. One of the most practical ways we can do that is through a life of giving.

Choosing a Path of Generosity

In recent years, social scientists have learned a great deal about happiness. One of the surprising findings is that the things we believe will make us happy often don't. According to Harvard psychologist Daniel Gilbert, people who win the lottery enjoy an initial spike of happiness. A year later, however, they've adjusted to their new circumstances and are no longer significantly happier than those who haven't won. (Another study found that accident victims suffering crippling disabilities were initially deeply unhappy, but just one month after becoming paraplegics, they were in fairly good spirits most of the time.[8])

But, psychologists indicate, some things actually *can* affect our happiness in an *enduring* way. One is to give our energy and finances to a cause larger and greater than ourselves.[9] Though we may be motivated at first by a sense of obligation or duty, we will soon discover great joy as we offer something of ourselves to a greater purpose. As we grow in dependence on God, choosing a path of humble simplicity and generosity, we remove the clutter that can accumulate in our relationships with God and others. We are thus free to live more fully and to invest more deeply in the things that truly stir our hearts. Paradoxically, our most enduring happiness does not come from what we gain but rather from what we give away, offering who we are and what we have to bless others.

> *Our most enduring happiness does not come from what we gain but rather from what we give away.*

Shane Claiborne witnessed this kind of happiness when he was working with Mother Teresa and the Sisters of Charity in Calcutta, India. While speaking at our church, he described how the mission used to throw street parties for beggar children, and how he wanted to celebrate the birthday of one of the kids he knew particularly well. It was about a hundred degrees, so he thought he'd get the boy an ice cream cone. Shane said:

> I had no idea if he had ever had ice cream before because he just stared at it and shook with excitement. And then his instinct was, "This is too good to keep to myself." So he immediately yelled to the other kids, "We've got ice cream! Everybody gets a lick." He lined them up and went down the line saying, "Your turn. Your turn." Then he got full circle back to me and he says, "Shane, you get a lick too." I've got this whole spit-phobia thing going on, so I kind of faked a lick and said, "Hmm, that's so good."

But that kid knew the secret. He knew the secret that the best thing to do with the best things in life is to give them away.

Though Shane's young friend in Calcutta may have never heard the words of Jesus, he understood from his life experience the truth of Jesus' teaching: we find our life by giving it away. Sometimes, we will be stirred to give away an ice cream cone, a beloved piece of art or furniture, or a vehicle. And sometimes, like monks when they join a monastery, we may be stirred to give everything.

Jon Pedley, a successful and wealthy businessman, used to live an extravagant lifestyle, driving luxury cars, taking exotic vacations, denying himself nothing—including alcohol, drugs, and sexual affairs. He describes his life as "utterly self-centered." Though he was living his dream, he was "still unhappy; something was missing." His chauffeur, knowing he was restless, encouraged him to attend a local church service. Pedley recalls: "It was different to anything else I had ever seen. . . . There was a confidence about [the congregation]. I was sure I had more money, I was sure I drove a bigger car and had been to more places and done more things. But they were more at peace." Pedley took an Alpha course, which helps people explore the Christian faith. "The last thing I wanted to do was become a Christian!" he laughs. But he surrendered his life to Christ. A week later he was with his then six-year-old son, who took his hand and said, "'Happy new you, Dad.' I said, 'What son?' And he said, 'You're like a brand-new person!'"

Pedley began giving away 15 percent of his earnings to

God's work. But increasingly, he felt there was more he could be doing. He went on a mission trip to Uganda and was overcome by both the poverty and the sacrificial generosity of the people. After only a few days of serving there, he received a bag of potatoes from the locals in gratitude for his work—a gift that was worth a fortune to them. He sensed God calling him to bring kids from the UK—who were on a downward spiral of addiction and self-hatred—to Africa for month-long, life-changing mission trips. Pedley put everything he owned up for sale: his idyllic sixteenth-century farmhouse complete with landscaped gardens, his successful consulting and marketing businesses, and his top-of-the-line Range Rover. He traded all these to live in a traditional mud hut in rural Uganda and start a mission to benefit the desperately poor. He helped by providing health care, clean drinking water, and better schools. He would also go on to foster the transformation of hundreds of young people in the UK who supported the project on the ground. "I've stopped chasing money and started serving the God that I love and the people he loves most—the materially poor in Uganda and the spiritually poor in the UK that we bring out here. It feels absolutely flipping fantastic!" As Jon Pedley began to feel deep contentment through his relationship with Christ, he was free to give joyfully and generously. Like the young boy in India, he is living the paradox of Jesus as he finds his life by losing it in service for God and others every day.

We may or may not feel compelled to give literally everything, as Jon Pedley has, but as we find ourselves satisfied with what Christ has done in our hearts, we will find ourselves joyfully giving our very best to God and others.

Your Real Advantage

Earlier, I mentioned that when I first became the pastor of Tenth Church, a faith community in the heart of Vancouver, it had cycled through twenty pastors (including associate pastors), in twenty years. Attendance had dwindled from more than a thousand during its glory years in the 1950s to the 100s. At a time when many churches were evacuating the city center in favor of the suburbs, a few of the elders of our church warned me that it might be too expensive to continue our church in the center of the city. When our original sanctuary, which had been built in 1938, deteriorated to the point that we had to close it down, our leadership questioned if we should stay put or sell the property and move further away from the urban center, where land was cheaper.

After a time of prayerful discernment, we decided that we would literally and figuratively stake our future in the heart of our city and rebuild where we were. When Vancouver won the bid to host the 2010 Winter Olympics, the cost of construction skyrocketed, and our project estimate ballooned from 2.3 million to 4 million dollars. Confident that we were called to remain where we were, our leadership invited our community to give generously. My wife, Sakiko, and I were newlyweds at the time, struggling to make ends meet. I recall a bill lying on our kitchen table and Sakiko asking me, "How will we pay this?" because we didn't have enough money in our bank account.

But in the midst of this financially challenging time, Sakiko and I committed to giving the equivalent of 50 percent of our yearly income, over and above our regular tithing—even though it felt like a big stretch. At the end of the church's three-year campaign, we not only reached our goal but exceeded it. Along with the many other people in our community who gave joyfully and sacrificially, we felt a burst of gratitude and happiness. We were able to rebuild and remain in our current location and have since opened two additional Tenth sites in different parts of our city.

When we choose to live simply and give generously, some people may wonder if we are being wise. For example, Jon Pedley was told he wasn't being prudent when he sold his business and country estate for the sake of God's mission. Well-meaning people have also questioned the prudence of my giving habits. Accountants—who have my best interests at heart—have cautioned me not to go overboard in charitable giving, since there's no longer a tax advantage to giving more.

Yet with God, there is never a disadvantage to being generous. Though generosity may not make sense logically, it makes sense *theo*-logically, because as I know from experience and as Scripture tells us over and over again, God is faithful. When we trust and experience God's loving faithfulness to provide exactly what we need, at exactly the right moment, time and time again, our lives will be marked by an abiding peace, gratitude, and joyful contentment in God.

> *Though generosity may not make sense logically, it makes sense* theo-*logically, because God is faithful.*

While I believe that saving a certain amount is prudent (I am Japanese, after all!), I also believe that we don't need to stockpile fearfully for our future. Rather, we can prayerfully determine how much we need to live on in a given year as a family and give the rest away. When my first book was approved for publication, I shared the news with a close friend over coffee and mentioned that I was setting up the contract so that the proceeds from any book sales would help support World Vision and similar organizations that provide for vulnerable children.

My friend leaned over and whispered, "But what if it becomes a bestseller?"

"It won't—it's about an obscure monastic rule of life," I reasoned.

"You never know . . . you may regret this."

Though the book did become an international bestseller, I have no regrets. We were recently able to give two six-figure gifts.*

And I enjoyed it so much, I'm doing it again. All proceeds from the book you are holding in your hands will also be given to missions that support vulnerable children.

I don't believe I've lost anything by directing my earnings to missions. In fact, I'm getting my money's worth, because the cash is working for more people, and my needs are still being met. And while I am stirred to support the plight of vulnerable children, you may feel passionate about ending human trafficking, preventing violence against women, or caring for the well-being of creation. Your greatest, most enduring happiness will not come from your material possessions or financial security, but from devoting your time, talent, and treasure to something bigger than yourself. As you live this adventure, you will learn, like Jesus, to depend on God for your needs and to identify more compassionately with the needs of the poor. But in God's economy, you're not giving away your advantage. For Jesus

---

* This includes accompanying gifts from our faith community in Vancouver: one to support World Vision's program to end violence against children in Cambodia and another gift to help a mission that serves orphans in Cambodia establish the first Christian camp in the history of the country.

clearly taught that if we seek God first, all that we need and more will be added to us, both in this life and the life to come (Matthew 6:33).

I pray you will grow content in God and trust in his loving faithfulness—and know you can absolutely bet on God. That is a great way to live and the best way to die. As the Heidelberg Catechism says, "Our only real hope in life and death is Jesus Christ."

Questions *for* Reflection
and Discussion

———————◇———————

1. How does knowing Jesus open the door to a life of greater simplicity?
2. What is the relationship between gratitude and living simply?
3. What, if any, fears do you have about moving toward a simpler lifestyle?
4. List ten things in your home (clothes, books, sporting equipment, etc.) that you have not used in the last year. How would you feel about giving these things away?
5. What are the gifts of a simpler lifestyle?
6. Have you experienced Jesus' upside-down teaching that you will find life by losing it? If so, describe one such experience.
7. How might living simply enable you to bless others?

Prayer

Lord, free me from a sense of scarcity. Help me be content with all you've given. Grow within me a generous spirit toward my neighbor. May I seek the good of others and honor your name in all I do. Amen.[10]

Chapter 8

SERVANTHOOD
Pouring Ourselves Out for Others

*Whoever wants to become great among you must be
your servant.*

–MATTHEW 20:26

I n college I majored in business economics and planned to work
in the corporate world upon graduation. But in the back of my
mind, I had a sense that God might call me to enter the so-called
"Christian ministry," perhaps as a pastor or missionary. So during
my freshman year, when I heard that the world-renowned evangelist Billy Graham was coming to our campus, I went to hear
him speak. Afterward, I walked to the front of the auditorium
to meet him, figuring the connection might help me out some-
day. We shook hands, exchanged a few words, and I went off to
class—marveling about the fact that I had just met Billy Graham.

After graduation, I ended up working in the corporate world
for a couple of years. But when my desire to pursue vocational
ministry grew, I headed off to seminary, and after completing
my theological degree, I moved to Los Angeles to help start a
new church. There I began mentoring a young lawyer. One day

he asked me, "Do you want to have lunch with the VP?" "The VP of *what*?" I replied. "The Vice President of the United States, Al Gore." (My friend had done an internship under Gore at the White House.) Unexpectedly, I was able to meet Vice President Gore, who at the time was planning to run for president. Like so many ambitious young people with a hungry Striving Adam, I was eager to meet influential leaders who could advise me or open doors for me. My early years of work and ministry were driven by the premise, "It's not *what* you know that counts, but *who* you know."

Yet over time Jesus Christ has upended my values by his teaching that true greatness is not about ascending to the top of the social hierarchy, but rather taking the place of a humble, lowly servant. Jesus modeled this posture the night before he went to the cross. On what the poet John Donne calls "the world's last night," Jesus gathered some of his closest students in an upper room in Jerusalem to share a meal with them. Jesus "knew that the hour had come for him to leave this world" (John 13:1); the following day he would be nailed to a cross. On this last night, when death was imminent, Jesus revealed what he prized most: servanthood.

Although Jesus' apprentices had been with him for three years, they were still confused about the true nature of his mission. On the previous Sunday, Jesus had come into Jerusalem riding on a donkey, and a large crowd of people had lined the streets. They cried out, "Hosanna to the son of David," believing that God would save them through a great king like David. Today, we see similar red-carpet treatment in the United States when a promising, charismatic political leader is officially introduced as a party's presidential candidate.

Jesus' students were hoping he would ride that wave of popularity until he was elevated to the throne as king and Messiah. They fantasized about the kind of cabinet positions they would hold in Jesus' administration, jockeying for status and arguing about who would have the most powerful and prestigious roles (Luke 22:24). Imagine then the dilemma when, upon entering the upper room in Jerusalem to share the Passover meal with Jesus that evening, they discovered that there was no servant to wash their feet.

To understand the significance of this omission, you need to know that the roads of ancient Palestine were not paved, so people's bare or sandaled feet became quite dusty. Donkeys, stray dogs, and other animals traveled the same roads. What's more, homes in ancient Palestine did not have modern toilets, so people spilled their waste into the streets. Hence travelers' feet also became soiled with animal or human excrement. Foot washing was a necessity, but it was considered such a menial task that Jewish households assigned the duty to a Gentile slave, woman, or child. Normally, a dinner host hired a slave to wash the feet of the guests.

Partway through the evening meal, Jesus, whom the disciples called "master," suddenly removed his outer clothing and wrapped a towel around his waist. He poured water into a basin, began to wash his students' feet, and then dry them with a towel (John 13:4). Everyone was shocked, and Simon Peter exclaimed, "You shall never wash my feet!" (v. 8). Jesus' act was unprecedented—there is no record in antiquity of a rabbi stooping to wash the feet of his students. In fact, such an action would have been considered "unclean" according to the Jewish purity code, and therefore not permissible.

As a contemporary window into this shocking scenario, imagine that a writer, speaker, or entertainer whom you greatly admire comes to your town to give a speech. A friend arranges to get you a front-row ticket for the event. After the presentation, you bump into your hero, and you say, "I'm a really big fan of yours."

"What do you like about my work?" your hero asks.

Even though you're quite nervous, your thoughts focus like a laser, and you express how much this person's work has meant to you in a clear and eloquent way.

Then the celebrity says, "I'm staying at a nice hotel here, but I've been on the road for weeks, and I'm tired of eating at restaurants. I don't want to impose, but I'm wondering if I might come to your house for dinner before I leave town." Though you wonder if you are dreaming, you say, "How about tomorrow night?"

You invite a circle of your best and most presentable friends. At the appointed time, your guest of honor arrives, and everyone enjoys wine and appetizers until dinner is ready. As you all take your places around the table, your honored guest interrupts: "Before we eat, I would like to do something for you." After an awkward pause, the celebrity says, "I'd like to clean your toilet."[1]

If you can imagine the cringe factor that you and everyone else around the table would be feeling in that moment, you can appreciate how Jesus' disciples must have felt as Jesus began to wash their feet. It's no wonder that Peter declared, "No Lord, *you* shall never wash my feet."

Scripture tells us that Jesus Christ was God in human flesh (John 1:1, 14), and so, like no other human being before or since, he embodied true greatness. In this moving portrait, we see that the greatest person of all time revealed God's true character by humbly serving those around him. In Philippians 2, we read that although Jesus was in very nature God, he didn't use his status as God for his own *selfish advantage*. Instead, he poured himself out to serve others. Some translations render the Greek, "Jesus emptied himself," but the most accurate translations emphasize that "Jesus poured himself out" like water to serve others. This is a quintessential image for the living God. The gods of the ancient world were capricious, vindictive, and self-serving, but the one true God of the universe—the God we see in Jesus Christ—*serves*.

Some preachers suggest that Jesus gave up his power, but the truth is that he was able to serve precisely *because* he knew how powerful he was.[2] According to the Gospel of John, Jesus *knew* that the Father had put all things under his power and that he had come from God and was returning to God. *Because of this confidence* he was able to humble himself by washing the feet of those he "loved . . . to the end" (John 13:1). *Because* Jesus knew that he was loved and cherished by his Father, he had the strength to give up his *privilege*—not his power—as the most important person in the room. In serving his students that night, Jesus foreshadowed how he would serve the entire world in an even greater way the next day, as he offered his life for us on the cross. He bore our sin and shame so that we could experience forgiveness for our sins and receive fullness of life, now and in the world to come.

> *The one true God of the universe—the God we see in Jesus Christ*—serves.

Humble Acts of Hidden Service

When we feel insecure, we tend to posture, brag, or name-drop, attempting to make ourselves appear smarter or better than we are. But when we feel secure, loved, and cherished—when we remember whose we are—we are energized to serve others with humility and generosity. In the spiritual classic *Celebration of Discipline*, Richard Foster writes, "More than any other single way, the grace of humility is worked into our lives through the discipline of service. . . . Nothing disciplines the inordinate desires of the flesh like service, and nothing transforms the desires of the flesh like serving in hiddenness. The flesh whines against service, but screams against hidden service. It strains and pulls for honor and recognition."[3]

The late Brennan Manning, author of *The Ragamuffin Gospel*, was a former alcoholic who wrestled with feelings of insecurity, and yet he knew that he was deeply loved by God. He also knew the power of humble acts of service. He describes how one day, while waiting to catch a plane at the Atlanta airport, he sat down in a chair where black men usually shine white men's shoes. As an elderly black man began to shine Brennan's shoes, Brennan felt stirred to pay the man, tip him, and then reverse the roles.

When Brennan's shoes were finished, he stood up, and said, "Now sir, I would like to shine *your* shoes." The black man cringed, stepped back, and said, "You are going to do *what*?" Brennan replied, "I'd like to shine your shoes. Please. You sit right here. How would you like them done?" The black man began to cry, and said, "No white man ever talked to me like this before." Brennan was empowered to give up his privilege as a successful white man and serve a poor black man not only because he understood the feelings of shame and insecurity from his struggle with alcoholism, but also because he knew the astonishing power of being loved by God.

We also see the power of humble acts of service in the life of

Dorothy Day, the founder of the Catholic Worker movement. Day started out as a young, sexually active Bohemian writer in New York City during the 1920s. After giving birth to a baby girl—an experience that filled her with wonder, awe, and gratitude—she converted to Christianity. Day eventually became a deeply respected and powerful advocate for social justice, including women's and worker's rights. She also founded the influential newspaper the *Catholic Worker*, which at one point had a circulation of 150,000—a huge number for that era.[4]

Although Day was remarkably talented and creative, she spent most days at a bread and soup line, serving the poor and mentally disabled. Rather than visiting homeless shelters and then retreating to the comfort of her own home, Day lived in one of the hospitality houses herself. Because many people came to admire Day's work, she was aware of the temptation to feel self-righteous and knew that pride was lurking around every corner.[5] Part of what kept her from becoming vain was her engagement in humble acts of service every day. Though Day loved the poor, she had a writer's personality and was somewhat aloof, often craving solitude. But almost all day, every day, she pushed herself to be with those who had mental disabilities or suffered from alcoholism. Though the guests could be rude and vulgar, she made herself sit at the table and listen respectfully to the person across from her, even if that person was drunk and incoherent. Even after her memoir *A Long Loneliness* became a bestseller, catapulting her into fame, she remained humble and rooted in love through her humble acts of service.

In our struggle against vanity, feelings of entitlement, or an exaggerated sense of our own importance, humble acts of hidden service can help counter our pride and overweening ambition.

In his insightful book *Playing God: Redeeming the Gift of Power*, Andy Crouch, a Christian journalist, describes how his work takes him away from home several times a month. The hours preceding a trip are often consumed with making last-minute preparations for meetings or speeches. The last thing on his mind is "the mundane maintenance of his family life that will have to continue along the way." Yet while he is being treated with "absurd courtesy" and "showered with the accoutrements of power"—the wireless microphones that amplify his voice, the gracious introductions that amplify his accomplishments, the always polite and frequently enthusiastic applause, the meals out with old and new friends—there will still be dishes accumulating in the kitchen. So in the final minutes before leaving for the airport, one of his personal disciplines is to do all the dishes—sometimes while a taxi is waiting outside his house. He recalls, "Many times I have torn myself away from revising a talk, tweaking a set of presentation slides in order to plunge my hands into hot soapy water and deal with the dishes from last night, or to be honest *last week's* dinner." He writes:

> The honest truth is that not once have I ever felt any reason to regret my time spent serving my family in this way. On the other hand, when [I've] left a sink full of dishes behind in self-imposed hurry, I've been haunted by regret and the painful awareness of how little I trust God and how thin my love for my family is.[6]

Like Andy, I travel on a regular basis. I am a fairly messy guy, but for the sake of my wife and family, I try to be a little bit neater. (My wife will find that sentence perplexing!) But when I am staying at a hotel, I act like a single person again in that any concern for neatness falls away. I walk into my room, toss my jacket and other clothes onto the couch, and spread my books and speaking notes across the desk.

But when I'm about to leave my hotel for the airport, I cram my belongings into my carry-on and then quickly clean the hotel room, wiping down the bottom of the bathtub, placing the towels I've used over the wall of the bathtub, sponging off the counter, and sliding any furniture I've moved back into place.

I figure that the woman cleaning my hotel room must be very busy, and perhaps her life is full of stress, and so I want my room to be the easiest room she will clean that day. This very small gesture reminds me that I am not a star but a servant.

Seeking a Cross-Shaped Life

When someone told Ruth Martin, a physician and medical researcher in our faith community, about a job in a prison medical clinic, she initially resisted, because she felt it would be the lowest prestige job for a doctor. Yet after visiting a medical clinic in one of British Columbia's prisons, she knew she had found her calling. Since that time, she has become a courageous advocate for the health of women in prison. By marshaling compelling medical evidence to demonstrate the importance of mother-infant bonding (because it serves the future interests of children), she has helped infants born to imprisoned women remain with their mothers so they can develop healthy attachments.

About half of the women she works with are indigenous, First Nations people, and most have struggled with addictions to alcohol or drugs. Many of us assume that addicted people have made irresponsible choices. But as Ruth listened to the women's histories—the physical and sexual abuse they endured as children, young teenagers, and women—she says: "I would put my pen down and listen, and I realized that if I had been dealt the same cards, I might have been sitting in their chair. I would often place the Kleenex box close to the woman who was sharing her history, but also close enough to me that I could reach for a Kleenex for myself."

In her acceptance speech for the Governor General's Award (the highest civilian honor in Canada) for her outstanding contribution in helping to secure equality for women and girls in our country, she said, "I am humbled to be chosen for this award . . ." The word *humbled*, of course, can sound like the polite thing to say, but for Ruth there was nothing insincere about it. Ruth realized that if it weren't for circumstances beyond her control—the family she was born into, the community in which she was raised, her access to higher education, and many other factors—she might not have had such a fortunate life.

When we expose ourselves to those who are suffering—be it through our career, volunteer work, a mission trip, or the care-giving for a disabled loved one—we begin to realize that our lives could have looked very different. We become aware that we have benefited by winning a kind of lottery. These illuminating experiences fill us with Striving Adam's passion to make the most of our life and Soulful Adam's gratitude and humility to serve others and honor the Giver of all good gifts.

Last summer, I visited Nagasaki, Japan, where twenty-six Japanese martyrs were crucified for their faith in Christ on February 5, 1597. Over the course of a month, they were forced to trek from Kyoto to Nagasaki, a journey of about six hundred miles. When they arrived on the hill where they were to be crucified, one among them wasn't given a cross because he was only twelve years old. The boy asked, "Where is my cross?" So he became the twenty-sixth martyr.

When we follow Jesus Christ, our lives may flourish. But we must never forget the way of Jesus is also shaped literally and figuratively by the cross. As some theologians put it, we are called to a "cruciform" way of life. This doesn't mean, of course, that each of us will die a literal martyr's death, such as those sixteenth-century Japanese martyrs or the twenty-one Egyptians martyred in Libya in February 2015. But Jesus teaches that if we want to be his students, we are called to take up our cross daily and follow him.

With the twelve-year-old Japanese boy, we are called to ask, "Where is my cross?" How can we lay down our lives in self-giving love for others? When we choose humble acts of service each day, we take up our cross and follow the way of Jesus.

> *The way of Jesus is shaped literally and figuratively by the cross. We are called to a "cruciform" way of life.*

What does taking up the cross of Jesus look like for *you*? It might mean first *recalling you are the beloved* and then serving and caring for a sick friend, a child, an aging parent, grandparent, or in-law, or member of your small group. It might involve bringing a meal to someone who is hungry, grieving, or lonely, or listening to someone share his or her burdens, or caring for a homeless person through a shelter ministry in your city. The true greatness modeled by Jesus comes not from hobnobbing with the next Billy Graham or the Vice President of the United States but in surrendering our privileges as we serve others. If, like Jesus, we feel a sense of power because we know we are loved by our Father, and we know where we have come from and where we are going, then we can live a truly great life in God's economy—one in which we humbly serve one another and help to make our world a place that reflects the values of our Servant-King.

Questions *for* Reflection
and Discussion

———◆———

1. How does recognizing the power that God has given us free us to serve others?
2. How does serving cultivate humility?
3. Like Ruth Martin, do you ever feel that you won the "lottery" because of your life circumstances? If so, does this inspire you to live in a particular way?
4. How might God be calling you to live a cruciform life?

Prayer

Jesus, you are the way, the truth, and the life. You have called me to love you with all my heart, soul, mind, and strength—and to love my neighbor as myself. Help me embrace this call by filling me with your love. May your humble sacrifice on the cross empower me to serve others.

Chapter 9

FRIENDSHIP

The Art of Mutual Encouragement

There is nothing in this world so precious as a faithful friend and no scales can measure his [or her] excellence. A faithful friend is a sturdy shelter, a fortified palace. . . . This is truly a gift from God and clearly more than we deserve.[1]

—GREGORY OF NAZIANZUS

During my early twenties, while I was working for Sony in Tokyo, a friend invited me to celebrate Christmas Eve with him and his uncle, who was a member of the *Yakuza*, the Japanese mafia. I agreed. I planned to invite his uncle to a Christmas Eve service, hoping he'd convert to Christianity.

When I met my friend's uncle, I immediately noticed that his little finger was cut off halfway down. I knew that if you're part of the Japanese mafia and you make some kind of mistake, you lose a finger. If you screw up a bunch of times, you're going to have a lot of missing fingers. But I've also heard that if you're stuck in traffic and someone with a missing finger or two puts his hand out the window, the traffic will part as it would for an ambulance with a blaring siren. I also noticed that my friend's uncle had a strikingly attractive girlfriend, and I found myself wondering why gangsters get the best-looking girls. He also had a dynamic personality, a good sense of humor, and treated us to a sumptuous dinner.

As the night went on, I began to glamorize his lifestyle, and I thought that perhaps I should get his number in case I ever needed some help from a gangster in the future. After all, I reasoned, if anyone ever hassled me, he could utter the Japanese equivalent to, "You'll be sleeping with the fishes," from *The Godfather*. Originally, I had been hoping to have a good influence on him. But even though he did come to a late-night Christmas Eve service, he didn't convert—and he ended up having more influence on *me* than I did on him.

Thankfully, he wasn't the only person to influence my thinking at that time. During that same period of my life in Tokyo, I was making a lot more money than I ever had before. I was single and interacting with a wide range of people, including the occasional woman who would subtly let me know she was open to "hooking up." Because I wanted to live a life faithful to Christ, I began spending time with a Christian friend who shared a mutual desire to honor God. As our schedules allowed, we would go on walks and talk about the temptations we were facing in the areas of money and sex. Simply being in each other's presence as young men who wanted to live with integrity before God gave us the strength to pursue a path of purity. But I know myself well enough to realize that if I had been spending most of my time with Yakuza gangsters or people who thought it was cool to hook up with multiple partners, I could have been influenced in a different direction. Who we spend time with—and the friendships we develop—influence us more than we realize.

Friendships of Influence

Scientists have discovered that human beings tend to imitate one another. Our brains have specialized cells called mirror neurons that cause us to mimic what other people are doing. For example, if you're at a party and your conversation partner grabs some chips from a bowl, you may find yourself unconsciously mirroring her behavior and reaching for the chips—even if you're not particularly hungry. If your conversation partner crosses his arms, moments later you may unconsciously cross your arms as well. These mirror neurons also mimic other people's feelings. When someone walks into the office in a sour mood, you feel like *you* could use some chocolate to lift you up. Or if you walk into a room where someone is laughing, you will most likely feel a smile cross your face—even if you don't know what's so funny. Television sitcoms use laugh tracks because they know that if you hear other people laughing (even a recording), you are more likely to laugh yourself.[2]

Earlier, I introduced you to the story of Augustine of Hippo. Augustine was also aware that friendships can have positive or negative effects on us, causing us to do things we might not do on our own. His desire to be accepted by his peers as a child led him to join his friends in stealing pears from a neighbor's tree. As an adult, Augustine realized that he would not have stolen the pears if he had been by himself, and he reflected on the possible negative influence of friendship.[3] But he was also aware that friendship could ennoble us. In his spiritual autobiography *Confessions*, he wrote, "Human friendship is a nest of love and gentleness."[4]

According to the philosopher René Girard, not only do we imitate other people's physical actions and emotions, but we also unconsciously mimic their desires.[5] Desires are contagious. However, unlike contracting a cold or flu virus from being in random contact with a coworker or a cashier at a grocery store, the transmission of desires and values doesn't work as indiscriminately. Our *relationship* to the person determines how much we will be influenced by them. The closer we are to someone and the more we respect them, the more they will influence us.[6]

And this influence can extend from tiny choices about what we will eat for lunch to big decisions that affect the trajectory of our lives. For example, during my friend Curtis Chang's freshman year at Harvard, he mapped out his life: he would become a professor of sociology, and he already knew the titles for his first three academic books. As a quintessentially Type-A person and the winner of the prestigious Rockefeller Scholarship,

> *Not only do we imitate other people's physical actions and emotions, but we also unconsciously mimic their desires. Desires are contagious.*

he had all the gifts to make this happen. But Curtis became friends with a group of Christians who were concerned about the plight of the poor. They held a mirror up to each other in a loving way, encouraging each other frequently but also confronting each other when necessary. These friends as well as a season of working alongside the poor in South Africa clarified what was most important in Curtis's life, which transformed his Striving Adam's worldly ambition into a much deeper sense of calling.

Curtis would go on to teach public policy at Harvard for a time and now teaches strategic planning at the School of International Service at American University in Washington, D.C. He also founded Consulting Within Reach, which helps the government and NGOs work with the poor. As one of

Curtis's Harvard friends shared with me: "His life has borne a beautiful kind of integrated fruit that's so much more than his little track could have imagined. Now he has a wide scope of authority and certain kinds of power, but it's handled in a totally different way from what it would have been if he hadn't had those kinds of friendships and formative experiences." Curtis's ambition is no longer in the service of his resumé and career path, but channeled for something far greater: a world that more reflects the justice and beauty of Jesus. With the help of the Holy Spirit, Curtis's life demonstrates a robust, ambitious Striving Adam that can live in synergy with a healthy, compassionate Soulful Adam. His friendships have helped him live out this holistic calling. Over the past three decades, Curtis has continued to nurture close friendships from his college days. Part of his weekly rhythm is to have a phone call with his friend Karl every Friday. They continue to hold up a mirror of mutual encouragement and accountability to one another.

Friendships of Resistance:
Swimming Against the Current

As Curtis's story reveals, the individuals or groups of people we choose to expose ourselves to can shape us in significant and often unanticipated ways. Not long ago, I recognized the striking influence of friendship while having lunch with a talented couple in our faith community. Simon has a Master's Degree in international development, and Shannon is a hydrogeologist with a PhD in Environmental Studies, with a focus on providing clean water for people in the developing world.

They shared with me that they had recently sold their condo in Vancouver and were about to move to the Sudan to serve with an organization that provides clean water to impoverished communities.

I asked if they had any hesitation about leaving the familiar comforts of Vancouver and moving to Africa. Simon replied, "So many people in our society are consumed with accumulating money and material possessions. You know the saying, 'Dead fish move with the current, live fish swim against the current'? By God's grace, we're live fish, and so we want to swim against the current of our culture."

Because they will be serving in a region where extreme violence is common, they have been trained in how to respond when someone covers your face with a mask and takes you hostage. "It's not the kind of place where we could raise kids," Shannon told me. "We are in our early thirties. Many of our peers are starting to have kids, but because we cannot have young children where we will be serving, we're okay with not having kids of our own."

Simon said, "If we're called to serve in the Sudan, we might be among those who are called to lay down our lives literally. We wouldn't do anything stupid to make it happen unnecessarily, but if we were called to make that sacrifice, we'd be okay with that."

When I asked them how they had formed these convictions, Simon replied, "I meet regularly with a group of three guys. One of the guys in our group says, 'I see my life as a short-term mission trip and then I'm going home,' and we've caught that."

The people we associate with can profoundly influence our vision. God can use our friends to transform our desires, so that we are not ambitious for ambition itself, but rather ambitious to serve a higher calling. When we were younger, we may have been attracted to friends who were cool, popular, smart, or could open doors for us. A recent survey of the most important life goals for millennials revealed that over 80 percent aimed to get rich and 50 percent hoped to become famous.[7] But does *this kind* of ambition help us live better, more fulfilled lives?

The connection between the quality of our relationships and our sense of fulfillment is highlighted in a unique study by the Harvard Study of Adult Development. This project has tracked the lives of 724 men over the course of nearly eighty years, asking them about their work, home life, health, and happiness year after year.[8] And since 1938, the researchers have tracked the lives of two groups of men. The first group were sophomores at Harvard. They finished college during World War II, and most of them went off to serve in the war, then returned to become doctors or lawyers. One became the president of the United States. The second group were from some of the most troubled and disadvantaged families in Boston. These young men also served in the war and then went on to become factory workers and bricklayers.

At the time of this writing, nearly fifty of the original men, now mostly in their nineties, are still alive and participating in the study. According to Robert Waldinger, the current head of the research project, the clearest message from the eighty-year study is that good relationships keep us healthier and happier. The research shows that social connections help us flourish, and loneliness kills. It turns out that people who are socially connected to family, friends, and a community have stronger immune systems, are more joyful, and live longer than those who are less connected. What is important is not the number of friends you have or whether or not you are in a "committed relationship." In fact, a toxic marriage is hazardous to your health. It's the *quality* of our relationships that matter.

We also know from Scripture that good relationships foster a healthier spiritual life. Proverbs 13:20 says, "Walk with the wise and become wise, for a companion of fools suffers harm." Similarly, the ancient Greek philosopher Aristotle observed that true friendship is not based on what another person can do for you, nor how a person makes you feel, but on mutual respect and admiration, where people help one another cultivate virtue.[9]

If you are reading this book, you're probably not looking for friends whose primary pursuit is a nicer car, a larger house, more exotic vacations, or better schools for their kids, but rather soul friends who want to make God the central focus of their life. As we pursue these kinds of relationships, we will find ourselves growing in faith, devotion, kindness, justice, and generosity. As we spend time with people we admire, consciously or unconsciously, we will begin to bend our lives to mimic theirs. So how do we find and cultivate soul friendships that will help us keep God as the central focus of our lives? Here are a few simple suggestions.

Praying for Friendships of Mutual Encouragement

While many of us have probably prayed for a romantic relationship, we may not have thought about asking God to lead us to spiritual friendships. Scripture reveals how God drew people together in spiritual friendship, including Ruth and Naomi, David and Jonathan, Paul and Timothy, and Jesus and his disciples.

According to the Gospels, Jesus stayed up all night twice—most famously, in the garden of Gethsemane, on the night before his death on the cross (Luke 22:39–46). But at the beginning of his public ministry, he also prayed until dawn prior to calling his closest friends (Luke 6:12–16). The fact that Jesus spent that entire night asking God to guide him in the selection of the twelve disciples reveals how vital it was to discern who God had chosen for him.

In the same way, we can pray our way toward the friendships God has ordained for our mutual encouragement.

In the spiritual classic *The Four Loves*, C. S. Lewis elaborates on the words of Jesus in John 15:16, which describe the disciples' relationship with one another. Lewis observes: "In friendship . . . we think we have chosen our peers . . . But, for a Christian, there are, strictly speaking, no chances. A secret master of ceremonies has been at work. Christ, who said to the disciples, 'Ye have not chosen me, but I have chosen you,' can truly say to every group of Christian friends, 'Ye have not chosen one another but I have chosen you for one another.'"[10]

If you're not currently in a spiritual friendship that inspires you toward Christ and his call upon your life, pray about initiating a connection with someone who might become a friend on the journey. Consider inviting this person to get together for lunch or coffee so that you can begin to explore whether there is a mutual desire to meet (or talk by phone or Skype) on a regular basis for a season.

Cultivating Friendships of
Mutual Encouragement

In our industrialized Western world, most people don't value friendships above their career choices. As my former seminary professor Dr. Susan Phillips observes, people will move across the continent or to a foreign country to advance their careers, but rarely will they move somewhere simply because they have a friend in that part of the world, or seldom will they turn down a promotion requiring a transfer because they want to stay in proximity to a friend in their current city. We live in a society that values Striving Adam's career achievement and the accumulation of financial wealth more than Soulful Adam friendship. Perhaps this has been so in almost every age. The ancient Greek philosopher Socrates, writing in the fourth century BC, observes that although people say that there is no possession better than a good friend, most people concern themselves with acquiring houses, fields, cattle, and slaves.[11]

We are influenced by the Striving Adam's values of our society, which prioritize getting things done, over Soulful Adam's desire to cultivate relationships. When we have thirty minutes of discretionary time, many of us are more likely to use that time for something related to our work rather than investing in a relationship. After all, when we achieve something at work, we receive instant feedback, perhaps even in the form of a raise, promotion, or new contract.[12]

Or when we have a little free time, we may be inclined to use that time for social media or watching Netflix, which also promise immediate gratification. Cultivating relationships with friends and family members, by contrast, often requires years of investment, and we usually don't see immediate results. If you're a parent, for example, it can take twenty or thirty years or more before you can put your hands on your hips and say, "We raised pretty good kids!"

Furthermore, our friends and family members rarely shout the loudest to demand our attention, and so it can be tempting for us to place these relationships on the back burner. But if we neglect the people we ought to care about most, we may find that when crisis hits, and we need the support of our friends and family, we are alone.

> *Our friends and family members rarely shout the loudest to demand our attention, and so it can be tempting for us to place these relationships on the back burner.*

For most people, friendship does not feel like an urgent priority. But if friendships are truly important to us, we will take the initiative to cultivate them. It's one thing to say we value relationships, but this doesn't mean anything if we don't take action.

In my book *God in My Everything*, I describe creating a flexible rhythm of life that creates a container for new and existing relationships. For example, part of my rhythm of life includes being home by 5:30 p.m. so that there's enough daylight left to bike or throw a baseball with our young son, Joey. I also try to limit my evening work to three nights per week (with the exception of crunch times) so I can enjoy time with family and friends. In my line of work, I can be consumed by crisis after crisis, and so I aim to set aside one lunch per week to meet with someone with no agenda other than wanting to grow a relationship with that person.

As I noted earlier, I also observe a twenty-four-hour Sabbath.

This day regularly includes time with family and friends, either in person, by phone, or FaceTime if they are far away. And in terms of my yearly rhythm, I also set aside most of July and August, turning down any travel for speaking engagements during these summer holiday months, so that I can be more available for my family. By nature, I am so Type-A/Striving Adam oriented that I struggle to say no to attractive and meaningful work-related opportunities any time of the year, but I feel at peace, because I sense this is the right thing to do.

If you're a busy person, cultivating significant relationships will mean saying no to some things in order to make space for the "big rocks" of family and friends in the jar of your life.

Becoming the Friend We Long For

You may feel anxiety about spending too much of your time and energy on the treadmill of work at the expense of relationships. Perhaps you fear that at the end of your life, you'll be all alone because of such choices. But as a mentor of mine says, "If you *become* the friend your heart longs for, you'll *have* all the friends you need." And as the book of Proverbs says, a generous person has many friends (Proverbs 19:6). This, of course, isn't just about being generous with money, but also with the gifts of time, energy, attention, love, and care.

If you become *the friend your heart longs for, you'll* have *all the friends you need.*

We see this theme at work in *It's a Wonderful Life*, a favorite film I watch every Christmas. Though the film is set in the first half of the twentieth century, it continues to resonate with many people. The main character, George Bailey, is a banker who oversees a small savings and loan. When George's absentminded Uncle Billy misplaces eight thousand dollars of bank money (an enormous sum at that time), George is afraid that people will assume *he* stole the money or lost it on a high-risk gamble. He fears going to jail and facing a scandal that will cloud his life, and the accompanying shame that will befall his family. But in the darkest moment of his life, his friends come to his aid. Though George is financially poor, he discovers that he is rich in friendships. Because he is a friend to many people, he is surrounded by people who are eager to help him.

We all want to feel that in the darkest moments of our lives, we will be surrounded by friends.

So are we taking the initiative to invest in relationships with our friends and family? Hugh Black observes:

> We would like to get the good of our friends, without burdening ourselves with any responsibility about keeping them friends. The commonest mistake we make is that we spread our intercourse over a mass, and have no depth of heart left. We lament that we have no staunch and faithful friend, when we have really not expended the love which produces such. We want to reap where we have not sown.[13]

If we want to reap lasting friendships of mutual transformation, we need to sow into the lives of those people who have been woven into our lives. Alcuin, a medieval tutor and counselor to King Charlemagne, writes about friendship in a letter to the king: "The word 'friend' derives from 'custodian of the soul' [*amicus dicitur quasi animi custos*], that is, one who strives with the full commitment of loyalty to keep the soul of his friend intact."[14] We become "custodians of the soul" in our friendships when we ask each other vulnerable questions, such as:

What are some of your greatest challenges?
Where are you being tempted?
What are you finding especially encouraging?
How is your relationship with God?

If I have learned anything about the art of this kind of friendship, it has come by example. I know that I am only able to mentor younger pastors and leaders because I benefited from the mentoring and deep friendship of Leighton Ford, an older Christian minister. For more than two decades, he has been present for me during every crucial turning point of my life, along with many everyday moments. He has listened to my life in a way that has given me the courage to grow more transparent with my temptations and struggles and more honest about my hopes and fears.

If you want to grow in your capacity to listen to people's stories, you might consider seeking a mentor or a spiritual director. Spiritual direction has long been a common practice among Catholics, but Protestants are becoming increasingly familiar with this life-giving discipline.[15] A good spiritual director offers spiritual guidance and companionship to help us make sense of our faith journey.[16] As Susan Phillips says, a spiritual director will "hold you in a place of belovedness" and listen to you so intently that you feel safe enough to access deeper parts of your soul and hear God in fresh ways.[17] This precious gift of being genuinely heard will help you become more present to others.

Tony Campolo, a dynamic preacher and social activist, once told me that when he was teaching a sociology class at the University of Pennsylvania, he would ask, "How can a person become the ideal human being?" His students responded by saying that for someone to become an ideal person, he or she would have to associate closely with an ideal human being. Tony would then ask his students to list the character qualities of an ideal person, and they would offer "love," "wisdom," "loyalty," "courage," and so forth. When Tony would next ask if anyone knew someone who embodied all of these characteristics, silence would always follow. Finally, in a bold and prophetic way, Tony would say, "There's just one person who is like this: Jesus. If you become friends with Jesus, you can become like this."

As we deepen our friendships with Jesus Christ, we become the kind of friend our hearts long for and receive the friends God has for us.

Encouraging One Another to Love

In the previous chapter, I mentioned the memorial in Nagasaki, Japan, for the twenty-six martyrs who were crucified for their faith in Christ on February 5, 1597. Like the Roman Caesars centuries earlier, the Japanese Emperor Hideyoshi felt that Christians were a threat to the empire because they would not pledge absolute obedience to the emperor. So he passed an edict, making it a crime, punishable by death, for anyone to bow their knee to any other god except the emperor. As portrayed in Shusaku Endo's classic novel *Silence*, people were given a financial reward for information leading to the arrest of a Christian.

Twenty-four Christians who refused to renounce Christ and confess the emperor as Lord were forced to set out on foot from Kyoto to Nagasaki, a distance of more than six hundred miles. Anyone willing to deny Jesus Christ would have had their life spared, avoiding an excruciating death, but each pilgrim remained faithful to the end of the journey. Then two anonymous Christians who saw the twenty-four others walking toward Nagasaki were so deeply inspired by their faithfulness that they joined them, and so the twenty-four martyrs became the twenty-six.

How were these martyrs able to remain faithful, even when faithfulness meant death? Along that six-hundred-mile trek, which took about a month, the pilgrims were constantly encouraging each other to remain steadfast. The Christian faith was never meant to be practiced as a solo trek but rather as a team race.

Most of us will not face actual martyrdom for our faith in Christ, yet we still feel powerful forces conspiring to pull us away from our complete devotion to God. We may experience pressure to spend too much time on the treadmill of work. Or we may be tempted to seek our primary validation through our achievements or to compromise sexually. We can remain faithful to God and his calling on our lives when we intentionally walk with a fellow pilgrim or two, encouraging one another to stay true on our journey—even when the way is costly.

May we take to heart these words from the writer of the letter to the Hebrews: "Let us think of ways to motivate one another to acts of love and good works. And let us not neglect our meeting together, as some people do, but encourage one another, especially now that the day of his return is drawing near."[18]

Questions *for* Reflection and Discussion

1. Like Augustine, can you think of someone who influenced you for the worse? In what ways?
2. Has a friend ever influenced you toward God? In what ways?
3. What role do you think prayer might play in making friends?
4. Are there people who you sense God has brought into your life? And, if so, for what reason(s)?
5. Do you have a friend (or group of friends) who acts as a "custodian of the soul," someone to whom you can ask vulnerable questions?
6. How can you cultivate friendship(s) of mutual encouragement?

Prayer

Dear Lord,
Give me a few friends
who will love me for what I am,
and keep ever burning
before my wandering steps.[19]

Chapter 10

VOCATION

Discerning Our Sacred Calling

Before I can tell my life what I want to do with it,
I must listen to my life telling me who I am.[1]
–PARKER PALMER

When I was single and a new pastor in Vancouver, I occasionally traveled back to Japan to connect with friends I had made while working at Sony. On one such trip, I met a close friend on a private island to discuss a personal problem he was facing.

Before leaving for Japan, an elderly woman at our church approached me, tapped me on the shoulder, and said, "I am praying that you will meet your future wife on this trip." I brushed off her comment, explaining that I wouldn't be seeing anyone but an old friend. However, while in Japan, my friend decided to connect me with a close female friend of his from college. After that trip, she and I began a long-distance relationship. While our relationship was progressing, I recalled the elderly woman's prayer and realized that God had been speaking to me. Eventually, Sakiko and I were married.

When we spend time with God in prayer and deepen our relationship with him, we may not be guided in dramatic ways, but we will become more attentive to the small signs of guidance that he brings into our life—even if we only notice them as we look back.

In Leo Tolstoy's 1886 novella *The Death of Ivan Ilyich*, the main character (Ivan Ilyich) is a successful lawyer. Ivan grows up in a middle-class home, but while at law school in Russia, he learns about the customs of the rich and yearns to climb the social ladder. He has a starchy, serious older brother and a wild younger brother, but Ivan prides himself on being cheerful, capable, and dutiful—always doing what is right in the eyes of his authorities. He steadily climbs the ranks of his legal profession, and thanks to the favor of a friend, he is awarded a post as a judge.

His self-centered wife, Praskoyva, loathes him, and both his daughter, Lisa, and son, Vasya, are distant. Resentful, Ivan turns away from his family and absorbs himself completely in his work. One day, while hanging curtains in his fancy new home, he falls awkwardly on his side. As the pain grows worse, he notices a strange taste in his mouth. Although he's only forty-five years old, it becomes apparent that he is dying from the wound.

Weak and bedridden, Ivan reflects on the meaning of his life. At first, he feels that he does not deserve his suffering because he believes he has lived a good life.

Though he remembers many happy moments as a young boy, he realizes that as he has moved further away from his childhood and climbed the ladder of social success, he has become more unhappy. His professional success now feels trivial, and his family life and social interests seem fake.

While on his deathbed, the thought occurs to him, "Maybe I did not live as I ought to have done?"[2]

Suddenly, Ivan "feels a strong jolt in the chest and side," pushing him into the presence of a bright light.[3] His bitterness toward his family falls away, and he is filled with compassion. With a sigh and a burst of joy, Ivan stretches out and dies.

Tolstoy wrote this novella when he was in his mid-fifties as he reflected on the meaning of his own life. He had already published his great novels, *War and Peace* and *Anna Karenina*, and had become world famous and rich. Yet he had come to realize that his life was not congruent with God's values, but rather with those of society. As he reflected on his inevitable death, he questioned the validity of his restless desire to become more wealthy, powerful, and famous than others. He realized that it did not matter if he had vast tracts of land, owned three hundred horses, or was more famous than Pushkin or Shakespeare. He sought to find answers by contemplating the way of Jesus Christ, and this pursuit led him to reshape his priorities radically.

Unlike Ivan, who surrendered to the light of compassion and joy at the very end of his life, Tolstoy reexamined his life priorities *before* he died. As he contemplated the way of Christ, he discovered that Jesus offered him the paradox of finding his true life in God as he relinquished his grip on the life he had built for himself.

Can you see yourself on your deathbed, in the presence of the bright light that shone down on Ivan and illuminated Tolstoy's imagination, asking yourself, "Did I live the life I should have lived?" Though this may seem morbid, St. Ignatius of Loyola (who developed the prayer of examen discussed in chapter six) taught that it can be fruitful to imagine ourselves at the point of death, because it can help us clarify what we value most.

God will not ask us:

Did you dutifully do what is right in the eyes of your authorities?
Did you faithfully mirror the values of your society?
Did you achieve the highest possible status?
Did you live a good life?

Rather, God will invite us to reflect on the nature of our relationship with him and with the whole of creation.

Did you do my will?
Did you live the life I created you to live?
Did you become the person I created you to be?
Did you live a life of love with me and all that I created?

In the garden of Gethsemane, Jesus prayed, "I have brought you glory on earth by finishing the work you gave me to do" (John 17:4). But what enabled Jesus to live perfectly in his Father's will as he finished the work God gave him to do? Let's explore how he did this.

Discernment as Surrender

First, Jesus Christ completely surrendered to the will of God. At the beginning of his ministry, Jesus said, "The Son can do nothing by himself; he can only do what he sees his Father doing" (John 5:19). At the end of his ministry on earth, Jesus prayed, "Not my will, but yours be done" (Luke 22:42). This simple prayer embodied the whole of Jesus' life as he lived it in relationship with his Father, offering his life in obedience to the Father's ways and purposes.

We may feel hesitant to surrender completely to God's will because we are afraid of where our Maker might lead us. We want God to show us his hand *before* we decide whether to follow his plan, or we want to negotiate a counteroffer, or choose to follow our own path. Or we may think that once we climb a couple more mountains and reach a clearer vista of the horizon ahead, we'll be better prepared to make an informed decision. Usually, however, God reveals his will to us *as* we trust him and surrender to his purposes (Proverbs 3:5–6).

St. Ignatius of Loyola, our guide in the prayer of examen, outlines three degrees of humility as a helpful and challenging path of surrender to God's

> *God reveals his will to us as we trust him and surrender to his purposes.*

purpose for our lives. The *first degree* of humility is to be truly surrendered to God. We seek to love God so much that we do nothing to dishonor him nor violate what he desires as revealed in Scripture or our conscience. This initial surrender prepares us to be guided by God.

The *second degree* of humility is to be completely open-handed to God. When given the possibilities of riches or poverty, fame or obscurity, a long and healthy life or a short life of suffering, we are to be completely open to God's will. We seek to be as "indifferent" or detached as possible to our preferences in order to be completely free to do the will of God.

The *third degree* of humility is to lean toward poverty, obscurity, and a short life of suffering rather than riches, fame, and a healthy long life because this way reflects the path that Jesus Christ took. Though this may sound extreme—and I certainly don't live this way—the motive is not masochism but rather to free ourselves from an exaggerated sense of self-importance. Our desire is to identify with Christ as we might identify with a close friend or family member who is suffering.[4]

Depending on your temperament, this third degree of humility might be applied inappropriately or even abused. However, for those of us who tend to find our sense of validation through our Striving Adam achievements, Loyola's path of humility can liberate us from a worldly and superficial way of measuring success.

Yet surrendering to God and his purposes for our lives doesn't necessarily mean that we will live in quiet obscurity. Loyola himself was not only a prayerful Soulful Adam "contemplative" but also very much a Striving Adam activator. The order he founded, the Jesuits, are known as "contemplatives in action." Loyola and his colleagues would go on to found hundreds of universities, hospitals, and communities of spiritual transformation. By 1800, one-fifth of Europe was educated by Jesuit schools.[5]

Loyola, however, was not propelled by worldly ambition and vanity, but rather by a clear sense that God was moving him. He was once asked, "How would you feel if hundreds of your universities were forced to shut down?"

He replied, "I hope I wouldn't need more than five minutes to get over it."

Jesus' life on earth was both contemplative and active, private and public. Jesus spent the first 90 percent of his life in obscurity, and though he did not intentionally seek the spotlight, the last 10 percent of his life was quite public. Until he was thirty years old, he lived in relative quiet, but during his final three years, he healed the sick, fed the hungry, mentored his students, and preached to large crowds. He was neither attached to public acclaim nor fixated on obscurity. Likewise, we are called to embrace God's will fully—whatever it may be and wherever it may lead us.

God may well call us away from a place of power and prestige to walk a humbler path, for this is the path that the God of the universe embraced when he descended to earth that first Christmas and became a baby—one of us—in Jesus Christ. As Scripture says, although Jesus was rich, yet for our sake he became poor, so that through his poverty we might become rich (2 Corinthians 8:9).

During the beginning of the thirteenth century, Saint Francis of Assisi and Clare of Assisi, who both came from wealthy families, followed this path because they felt called by God to forsake their large financial legacies and pursue lives of poverty and generosity.

More recently, Henri Nouwen felt led to step away from the glittering prestige of a professorship at Harvard to live in obscurity among the mentally and physically disabled of a L'Arche community in Toronto.

Jesus may also call us onto such a path of downward social mobility.

And yet God may call some of us to a path of upward social mobility. In Scripture, God takes Joseph from a dungeon and establishes him as prime minister of Egypt. Esther, a member of a despised, vulnerable minority in Persia, providentially becomes the queen. The apostle Paul was ambitious not only before but also *after* he came to know Christ. Following his conversion, he helped catalyze a new movement that would eventually upend the Roman Empire.

Though Striving Adam's desire to do something great can be self-centered and superficial, it may also come from God.

Andy Crouch, a respected editor and author, served as the leader of InterVarsity Christian Fellowship at Harvard for a decade. In that role, he and his fellow ministry leaders felt that it was their duty to subvert the values Harvard embodied by encouraging students to renounce power, wealth, and privilege. People who came into contact with InterVarsity were encouraged to practice "downward mobility" and to turn their back on the "American Dream." They were exhorted to move into an inner-city slum or the developing world to serve humbly.

But one day, Andy found himself talking to an African-American student from the ghetto, who said, "When I came to Harvard, my church and entire community had a prayer service commissioning me to study here because I am the first person from my church and my family to go to an Ivy League school. I was commissioned by my whole community. If I tell them I'm taking my Harvard degree and moving back into the hood, and not becoming a doctor, or lawyer or engineer, I will have completely failed my community."[6]

This young man felt that he could honor God most—and bless his family and community—by pursuing a professional vocation, thereby demonstrating that a different way of life was possible. Of course, our society holds to a narrow definition of success: wealth, power, and fame. But Christians can also adopt a narrow definition of success if we suggest that the *only* or best way to serve God is by directly working with the poor or entering into vocational Christian ministry as a pastor or missionary. What matters most is that we respond to the calling God has for *us*, regardless of what it is or where it takes us.

In order to discern how God is calling us, we will need to exercise a redeemed Striving Adam and a restored Soulful Adam as we become new creatures in Christ—what we might call a unified Whole Adam. We will need to seek God's guidance about when to pull back and pursue a more obscure path and when to step up and reach out to contribute more visibly.

Discernment as Waiting on God

In the midst of a demanding season of public life, Jesus regularly took time to seek his Father: "At daybreak, Jesus went to a solitary place" (Luke 4:42); "Jesus often withdrew to lonely places and prayed" (Luke 5:16). If the Son of God, who was capable of perfect discernment, actively sought his Father for guidance, how much more imperative is it for us, given all our foibles and distractions, to pursue God for direction?

If we don't make space to listen to God, we won't be able to perceive the ways he is speaking to us. If we're distracted by competing voices and desires, we won't notice his leading.

> *If the Son of God actively sought his Father for guidance, how much more imperative is it for us?*

But as we spend time with God in prayer, attend to his ways in Scripture, and deepen our relationship with him, we will become more aware of the small signs of guidance that God brings into our lives through people, nature, events, or the stirrings of our hearts. Our capacity to sense God's direction can also grow through something we've read, the counsel of a wise friend, our life circumstances, or an increasing sense of peace. As we observed in chapter four, though prayer may involve our speaking, we can also take a posture of silent listening. As we attend to the presence of our Creator, we become more receptive to his voice and more attuned to the guidance of the Holy Spirit.

After completing seminary, two opportunities emerged for me: I could either pursue a junior leadership post with an international organization focused on developing young leaders around the world, or I could head to Southern California to start a new church with a friend. I didn't have a clear sense about where God was leading me.

During my discernment, I remember walking with my mentor, Leighton Ford, not far from the Lincoln Memorial in Washington, D.C., explaining to him my dilemma. He said, "If you have reflected on what choice to make and have prayed about it, but don't discern any clear 'answer' from God, then try to project where you most want to be at the end of your life and go through the door you want to go through and trust God to make it right."

When we are seeking what pleases God but don't have a clear sense of his specific guidance, we are free to choose the path that seems to coincide with the arc of our lives. Though sometimes we may feel led to wait for a path to emerge, that may not always be practical—such as when we have a job offer with a deadline. In such situations, we can ask, "What do our best selves most deeply want?"

We have the freedom to follow the path where our joy intersects with our intuitive sense of what will honor and please

God. As writer and theologian Frederick Buechner said, "Vocation is the place where our deep gladness meets the world's deep need."

Occasionally, when I seek God for direction concerning a big decision, God makes his will known in an especially vivid way. After working in the corporate world and then for a church start-up, I took a week to fast and pray as I sought God about where he might be leading me next. On day three of the fast, the words "Tenth Avenue Alliance Church" came clearly to mind, though I had no formal connection with this church. On day five of the fast, the words "senior pastor" came to mind.

But most of the time, I am not guided in such dramatic and compelling ways.

Discernment as the Joy of Heaven

If you were raised in a conservative religious tradition, you may think it worldly and vain to honor Striving Adam, working hard to advance your education or career in a way that might bring you into a place of prominence. Or, you might have been led to believe that God will call you to do something you dread or to a long "ought." But as C. S. Lewis said, "Joy is the serious business of heaven."[7] One of the clearest signs we are in the will of God is that we feel fully alive.

In most cases, our vocation will be consistent with the way God designed us. Often we can find vocational clues in our childhood, a season when nearly everyone can remember experiencing a sense of joyful freedom.

When my wife Sakiko was a young girl, she loved to write.

From the time she was in the fifth grade, she kept a journal. In the sixth grade, she was a winner of a writing contest in Japan; as a result, even though she was not a follower of Jesus at the time, she had the thrill of meeting Mother Teresa. After graduating from university in Tokyo, she worked in Japan as a magazine editor and then a book publisher.

When she moved to Canada after our marriage, she felt as though her vocation had been taken from her, since her skills as an editor didn't transfer into an English-speaking context.

But then she was approached by Word of Life, a Christian publishing house in Japan, and asked to translate a book into Japanese that sold surprisingly well. She has since been asked to translate other books, and she experiences a great deal of joy and fulfillment in this work. She feels like an important part of her vocation has been restored to her.

If we needed a higher income as a family, Sakiko would be inclined to work for a mainstream publishing house, as opposed to a Christian one, but she believes that she is called to help seed Japan with good Christian books.

Even though joy is an important sign that we are in God's will, finding our vocation isn't as simple as "following our bliss." If we are truly called to something, we will have some level of gifting that will actually help other people. When I was a boy, I loved playing ice hockey—but I don't do that for my work. No one would or should pay me to play hockey. Right now, our professional hockey team, the Canucks, could use some help on the ice, but it won't be coming from me! So as we contemplate our vocation, we can also ask ourselves, "What do I do well?" or "With some practice, what *could* I do well?"

Obviously, pursuing the joy of heaven is different from

asking what will confer the most status upon us or net us the most money.

Many people who are not happy in their work have chosen their vocation because of the status or money. A dentist I know has had a successful and lucrative practice for three decades. But she isn't happy with her vocational life because she felt pressured by her parents, who were immigrants to Canada, to pursue a profession that would earn her respect and generate a good income. Of course, many dentists, doctors, lawyers, and business professionals truly love what they do and find deep satisfaction in using their gifts to serve the common good. Others may enjoy the perks of their job, but they often feel stuck and may even resent the work itself.

Joy is not only a sign that we have found our vocation but also that we are going about our work in a life-giving, God-honoring way. Dr. Winnie Su, a member of our faith community, is a highly respected physician and professor of medicine in Vancouver. She is also married with three young children. She recently shared with me that there's a part of her that would love to be more involved in cutting-edge research and writing papers for medical journals. But she feels that would be overreaching at this stage in her life, because she would have to compromise her family

> *Joy is not only a sign that we have found our vocation but also that we are going about our work in a life-giving, God-honoring way.*

life and forfeit the gifts of teaching Sunday school and going on medical missions to impoverished communities in China.

When we pour so much time into our work that we begin to sacrifice our most important relationships and priorities, or when we lose joy because our work feels relentless, it's a sign that we are out of the will of God. We may be in the right job, but we may be going about it in the wrong way. St. Ignatius of Loyola would counsel us to pay attention to what is happening inside us and to attend to our consolations (joys) and desolations (frustrations and sorrows) as a way to discern whether we are over- (or under-) working.[8]

When You're Stuck in a Tough Job

We can also determine whether or not our work matters to us by asking ourselves if we would continue our work without any financial compensation if we became independently wealthy.

When I first came to our church, one of the key funds had a balance of zero dollars. The fact that I was prepared, if necessary, to accept the role with little or no compensation and pursue other work on the side to support myself was, to me, a sign that I really wanted to pursue this pastoral work. Each year during my evaluation by our board, I ask myself, *If I were independently wealthy, would I continue my work without compensation?* Because I continue to answer *yes*, I sense that I should stay at my post.

Similarly, we can ask ourselves if we would continue our work even if it didn't carry any status or prestige.

Sometimes we may need to work a job we don't love simply to pay the rent or put food on the table for our family, or because of our physical limitations or a tight job market. We might take on a less meaningful job to pay our bills but then devote our energy and passion to volunteer work. If a job feels oppressive, and we have an opportunity to take a more life-giving position, we are wise to accept the new job (1 Corinthians 7:21).

But when we find ourselves stuck for a while in a lousy job with no alternative, we may be able to find meaning in our work if we ask God to enliven our imaginations so that we can bring the gift of our uniqueness into our current situation.

I witnessed this a couple of years ago while traveling through Pearson International Airport in Toronto. As I was waiting in the security line early that morning, I encountered a lively and truly luminous security staff woman whose accent told me she was from somewhere in the Caribbean. She reminded me of a younger version of Whoopi Goldberg in her *Sister Act* roles. This woman moved up and down the line with the effusive, positive energy and spirit of a charismatic preacher from the Deep South, asking, "Do you have something to be thankful for?" "Is this going to be a good day for you?" "Do you have something to praise God for?" And there was nothing artificial or weird about it.

Interestingly, people began to wake up, smile, and nod their heads as this woman brought her unique, beautiful spirit to what otherwise might have been a tedious, perhaps even soul-crushing, job. It was by far the best and most memorable experience I've ever had in the security line!

We often think of vocation as our paid work, but biblically speaking, vocation is a calling to live as holy people, which literally means that we are "set apart for God." Part of this holy calling involves directly or indirectly serving the common good so that our world reflects more closely the values of the kingdom of our Lord.

We also have relational callings. Though people might say of me, "Ken is a pastor," my job consists of only about a third or fourth in my vocational priorities—even though I love pastoring. I'm also called to be a husband and a father. And while I find fulfillment in being a father, it's a "job" that's very challenging—and one I have less control over. I'm also called to love the people around me.

Earlier in this chapter, we reflected on Tolstoy, who discovered in his mid-fifties that he was not living by his own values, let alone God's, but by the fleeting and superficial values of the world around him. As he meditated on the way of Jesus Christ, he came to embrace his truer vocation as a human being, set apart by God to serve the common good in order to make the world a better place.

Regardless of your age, you can do the same.

One day, like Ivan Ilyich, you will come into the presence of the great light. On that day, God will not ask:

Have you conformed to the values of your age?
Have you achieved the greatest possible success by the terms
   of your society?

Instead, God will ask:

Did you fulfill my calling for your one precious life?

Not someone else's calling, but your own.

Because I often find myself looking sideways rather than upward to assess the success or failure of my life, comparing myself to peers in my field, I am drawn repeatedly to the passage at the end of John, after Jesus' resurrection. Jesus is walking with Peter along the beach, and Jesus says to Peter, "When you are old . . . someone else will dress you and lead you where you do not want to go" (John 21:18). Jesus is intimating that Peter will one day die a martyr's death. John, another of Jesus' students, is apparently walking behind them, eavesdropping. In a fit of annoyance, Peter turns around, points at John, and asks, "What about him?" Jesus responds, "What is that to you? You follow me" (v. 22).

When I am tempted to compare myself to someone who is more successful than I am, or seems to have an easier path, I hear Jesus saying, "What is that to *you*? *You* follow me."

When I stand before God on Judgment Day, God will not ask me, "Why didn't you pastor a church of twenty-five thousand people?" Because that is not God's call for my life—that's a call for another pastor.

As an old man, Rabbi Zushya once said, "When I enter the world to come, God will not ask me, 'Why were you not Moses?' but rather, 'Why were you not Zushya?'"

When I enter the world to come, the Living God will not ask me, "Why were you not Billy Graham?" (or Mother Teresa, or Joel Osteen), but rather, "Why were you not Ken?"

As the jazz musician Duke Ellington said, "It is better to be a Number One *Yourself* than a Number Two *Somebody Else*." So embrace who God called you to be and open your hands to tend the work God called you to do.

Questions *for* Reflection
and Discussion

1. What is the relationship between surrendering to God and receiving God's guidance?
2. What are some of the ways God speaks to you?
3. Are you ever tempted, or have you ever been tempted, toward a wrong vocational choice for vain reasons? Explain.
4. How much freedom do you think God encourages in our decision-making?
5. How does imagining our death foster clarity?
6. How is joy an indicator that we are in God's will?
7. What are some signs that you might be out of the will of God?

Prayer

Put me to what You will.
Rank me with whom You will.
Put me to doing, or put me to suffering.
Let me be employed for You, or laid aside for You.
Exalted for You, or brought low for You.
Let me be full, let me be empty.
Let me have all things, let me have nothing.
I freely and heartily yield all things to Your pleasure,
*   and disposal. Amen.*

–JOHN WESLEY

Chapter 11

REDEFINING
GREATNESS

Purity of heart is to will one thing.

–SØREN KIERKEGAARD

N ot long ago, I was listening to an interview on National Public Radio with a young woman named Taylor Rose. Describing her job as a chemist as boring, she had applied to be a contestant on a reality TV show called *Mars One*. According to Taylor, if everything goes as planned, on a still to be determined date, she and three other human beings will step into a rocket that will blast off to Mars. The rest of their lives will be televised, and they will become instant celebrities.

There is just one catch: they'll only have a one-way ticket to Mars. They're not coming back. More people may join the colony, but no one will ever come *back*.

The radio host asked Taylor, "But what if you get to Mars, and you find that it really sucks there?"

Taylor responded, "Yah, that would really suck, but I would know that my life had been about something bigger than just being born, living, paying the bills, and dying."

Redirecting Desire

In previous generations, most people felt that it was enough to put in an honest day's work and provide for their family or contribute in some quiet way to their community. In those eras, most folks felt there was a dignity to that simple, everyday existence. According to the Pew Research Center, fame used to rank low as one of life's ambitions for young people. A 1976 survey asked respondents to list their life goals, and fame ranked fifteenth out of sixteen. Today, more than half of young people report that being famous is one of their top personal goals.[1] More than ever before, individuals feel they need to be extraordinary, spectacular, and do something a lot of people notice—or at least get a lot of "likes" on their Facebook page, garner many Twitter and Instagram followers, or produce a video that goes viral.

When young children feel they are doing something special, they will say, "Look at me!" Adults don't say, "Look at me!" but inwardly we *do* say, "*Notice* me." We want to be recognized. Though this desire may be self-centered and vain, it is also part of what it means to be a human being, made in the image of God. When Jesus says we are not to parade our good deeds or accomplishments before others, but rather to live before an audience of one (Matthew 6:1–4), he is not denying our natural desire to be noticed—he is simply *redirecting* it. Jesus teaches us to live for the applause of our Father in heaven.

Of course, living for the applause of our Father in heaven is no small victory, since our natural instinct is to desire the praise of people more than the praise of God (John 12:43). But if we live for the approval of people, we will discover a gaping void in our hearts, because we can never get enough affirmation, and whatever human approval we do receive will leave us feeling emptier and emptier. When we find ourselves needing more and more of what gives us less and less, we are, of course, on the classical path toward addiction. If we are living for the applause of people, we will also discover that someone else is receiving louder or longer applause. When we compare ourselves to others, we will feel envious and miserable; comparing leads to despairing.

But if we live for the applause of our Father in heaven, who cherishes us, we will find that his affirmation nourishes us, fills us, and sustains us far longer than human acclaim. As we live for the approval of God alone, we become full and free.

Just before Jesus entered his public ministry, he spent forty days alone in the desert, seeking his Father in heaven, praying and fasting. At the end of that time, the Gospels tell us that the devil approached Jesus and said, "You look like you've lost weight (a modern paraphrase). Why don't you turn these stones into bread?" Part of the temptation, of course, was for Jesus to satiate his hunger pangs, but part of the temptation was surely to get Jesus to define himself by what he could produce—by his *success*. Jesus responded by saying, "It is written: Man shall not live by bread alone, but on every word that comes from the mouth of God."

Next, the devil came to Jesus and gave him a whirlwind tour of the planet, showing him all its wealth and splendor. He said, "Jesus, if you will bow down to me just once, I will give you the kingdoms of this world. I will give you the *biggest platform ever*." Jesus responded by saying, "It is written: Worship the Lord your God, and serve *him* only."

Finally, the devil said to Jesus, "If you really are the Son of

God, go to the highest point on the temple of Jerusalem, stand on its pinnacle for dramatic effect, and then leap off the top. Will not your Father in heaven dispatch an angel to swoop down and pick you up in its arms before your feet strike the ground? It will be *spectacular*. It will '*wow*' everyone—what a way to begin your ministry!" Jesus responded, "It is written: Do not put the Lord your God to the test."

Jesus resists and rejects the temptation to be defined by his success, to create the largest possible platform, and to do the spectacular. Instead, he chooses to live not for the praise of people but for the praise of God, his Father, alone (Matthew 4:1–11).

Redefining True Greatness

Jesus not only redirects our natural desire to be noticed, but he also redefines true greatness. Our society defines greatness as being big or spectacular, but in the story of the widow's gift, Jesus teaches that a small and obscure offering is even greater in God's eyes (Luke 21:1–4). Jesus teaches us that many of the things that are esteemed by our culture are despised by God, while many of the things that are overlooked or ignored by our culture are honored by God (Luke 16:15). In fact, Jesus defines the truly great—those blessed of his Father who will inherit the kingdom—as those who feed the hungry, give a drink to the thirsty, offer hospitality to the stranger, clothe the naked, visit the sick, and advocate on behalf of the oppressed (Matthew 25:34–36). These actions typically go entirely unnoticed by the larger world.

Jesus' definition of greatness seems upside down—but perhaps we should think of his way as right side up, and our world as upside down. Jesus embodied this definition of greatness by choosing to live 90 percent of his life on earth in complete obscurity. As my friend Zack Eswine observes, Jesus' life shows us that greatness and obscurity are not opposites.

When I was an undergraduate student, I was invited to attend a conference

> *Jesus's life shows us that greatness and obscurity are not opposites.*

in Amsterdam for younger emerging Christian leaders. It was hosted by Billy Graham, who at the time was the best known and most respected Protestant Christian leader in the world. In an interview, a reporter asked, "Mr. Graham, who do you think is the *greatest* Christian in the world, right now?"

Mr. Graham paused and responded, "You wouldn't know them, because they are living out in some jungle in Africa, in complete obscurity. You wouldn't even know their name."

Jesus tells us that many who are first in this world will be last in the world to come, and many who are last in this world will be first in the world to come (Luke 13:30). C. S. Lewis vividly imagines how this might play out in his spiritual classic *The Great Divorce*. In one scene, a man is being given a tour of heaven, where he sees a dazzling woman of astonishing beauty with a group of boys and girls, singing and playing instruments in her honor.

> Turning to his guide, he whispers, "Is it? . . .'" [In other words, was she featured in *People* as one of the fifty most beautiful people in the world?]
>
> The guide says, "'She's someone you have never heard of. Her name on Earth was Sarah Smith and she lived at Golder's Green.'"

"She seems to be . . . well, a person of great importance?"

"Aye. She is. But fame on earth and fame in heaven are two very different things."

"And who are these boys and girls who are dancing and throwing flowers before her?"

"They are her sons and daughters."

"She had many children."

"She had no children of her own. Every boy that met her became her son—even if it was only the boy that brought the meat to her back door. Every girl that met her was her daughter."

"Wasn't that a bit hard on their own parents?"

"No. There *are* those that steal other people's children. But her love was of a different kind. Those on whom it fell went back to their natural parents loving them more . . .

"And now the abundance of life she has in Christ flows over into all creation."[2]

As Lewis points out through this narrative, *fame on earth and fame in heaven are two very different things.* Many who are first now will be last in the world to come, and many who are last here in this world may be first in the world to come (Luke 13:30).

An unmarried woman who shows kindness to boys and girls, or a brother in a hovel in Haiti sharing his bread with his younger sister, or an obscure woman caring for her aging father-in-law might be first in the world to come. Jesus upends our assumptions about what is truly great. For in the kingdom of heaven obscurity and greatness are not opposites.

If you are a follower of Jesus Christ, you probably do not

believe that people's actual worth depends on their net worth or fame. But at some level perhaps, you believe that if you were truly great in God's eyes, you would do something on earth that would become widely known and recognized for a long time. However, in God's estimation, your life may be truly great even if you are never recognized or widely known for your accomplishments.

In the classic novel *Middlemarch*, author George Eliot (Mary Anne Evans) compares her central character, Dorothea Brooke, to Saint Teresa of Avila, a Catholic mystic who founded seventeen convents across Europe

In God's estimation, your life may be truly great even if you are never recognized or widely known for your accomplishments.

and wrote a widely read spiritual autobiography. Eliot observes that Teresa became a famous saint because she was born into a wealthy, influential family at a time when Europe was ripe for her deep spiritual wisdom. Then Eliot reflects on the many "Teresas" that have been born who found for themselves "no epic life," nor are remembered for "some long-recognizable deed."[3]

Dorothea Brook is such a woman. She is beautiful and well born but avoids displaying her wealth. Instead, she envisions redesigning dilapidated cottages for her uncle's impoverished tenants. But because of the way her life turns, her plans fail to be realized. Instead of marrying a wealthy landowner and enjoying a comfortable life of privilege, as she is expected to do, she ends up wedding an older, sickly clergyman, Edward Casaubon. She hopes to share in his intellectual life and ministry, but Casaubon proves to be cold, rigid, and narrow-minded, and her marriage is unhappy. He ends up dying within two years of their wedding. Dorothea eventually goes on to marry her late husband's cousin, who has no property and comes from a disgraced family line. People around her insist that she cannot be a "good woman" because her marriage is socially unacceptable.

Despite her critics, Dorothea matures and grows magnanimous, always giving people the benefit of the doubt. She brings out the best in people. Self-forgetful, she always thinks of others first and is exceedingly generous with her money. Dorothea's accomplishments "were not widely visible," for "Her full nature . . . spent itself in channels which had no great name on the earth . . . *But the effect of her being on those around her was incalculably diffusive: for the growing good of the world is partly dependent on unhistoric acts; and that things are not so ill with you and me as they might have been is half owing to the number who lived faithfully a hidden life, and rest in unvisited tombs.*"[4]

Likewise, we may not have long-recognizable deeds or be buried in tombs that are visited by many, but we too can live the quiet, hidden life of an everyday saint, knowing such a life is not hidden from God. God especially values things that are hidden, obscure, and overlooked. In the Sermon on the Mount, Jesus identifies truly blessed persons as those who recognize their essential poverty, which is their utter dependence on God (Matthew 5:3). He further describes truly blessed persons as those who hunger and thirst after righteousness—as ones who long to live in right relationship with God and people (Matthew 5:6). Recognizing our need for God and yearning to live well with God and people will likely be overlooked by others, but these desires are applauded by our Maker and will be rewarded greatly in his kingdom (Matthew 5:12).

Those who have a strong Striving Adam achievement orientation and a desire to be recognized for their accomplishments will be liberated by Jesus' definition of greatness. Even those who are led into a public role discover that their most significant and lasting works are almost always done in the private sphere, unnoticed by others.

Cultivating Eulogy Virtues

My dad, now in his early eighties, was recently hospitalized for pneumonia. Though he recovered, I wonder if he is nearing the end of his race, and this has caused me to reflect about his life.

He grew up in Japan after the war, at a time when the country was devastated and impoverished. His family could not afford to buy him books, but he loved to read, and so he'd go to the local bookstore without any money and ask for books. The bookstore owner was very kind and said, "You can take any books you want, and you can pay me when you get the money." So Dad was able to read books that he didn't have the money to buy.

After completing high school, he was admitted to the most prestigious private university in the country. After graduation, when very few Japanese could afford to study in North America, Dad studied at Columbia University in New York City. While a student at Columbia, he attended President John Kennedy's birthday party, a large celebration at Madison Square Garden, where Marilyn Monroe famously jumped out of a cake and sang "Happy Birthday." After college, Dad was hired as a broadcaster in London for the BBC. While we were living in England, he was invited to have tea with Queen Elizabeth. Later, when we had moved to Canada, he became a broadcaster for the CBC, and his radio program was ranked second in the world in its category. To borrow language from *New York Times* columnist David Brooks, Dad had pretty decent "resumé virtues," but he had even better "eulogy virtues" (meaning character qualities). He was a man of integrity, humility, and immense kindness. From this vantage point, his career accomplishments, in comparison to his character, feel like a feather on the scale.

Near the end of Dad's working life, because of budget cutbacks at the CBC, the Japanese broadcasting division was cut. Dad ended his working life walking the hallways and delivering mail in the French-speaking section of the broadcasting company (though he could only speak French haltingly). As I now reflect over Dad's life, that humiliating setback at the end of his career also feels like lint on the scale, since it has no bearing on my estimation of him. What matters most are not his professional accomplishments nor humiliations, but who he is.

I am a son, and I am also a father. As I think about our son, Joey, who is in second grade, I do hope that he continues to study beyond high school. I hope he does not have the distinction of being the first person in our family tree, in recent memory, not to go to college. But as I think about his future and look deep into my heart, I know that it really doesn't matter if Joey ever goes to a great university, or even if he goes to college at all. It doesn't really matter if he lands a really prestigious job. The only thing that really matters is if he awakens to a friendship with God, his Creator. And one day, if he has any social capital, financial resources, or talent, I hope he will use some of his gifts to serve people who are vulnerable. These eulogy virtues are the only things that matter, and I pray that with God's help he will cultivate them.

St. Dominic once said, "Death will kill a man, but the thought of death can save him or her." We saw this at work in the previous chapter, as Tolstoy reckoned with his own death through the character of Ivan Ilyich. When we come face to face with our own death, we realize that it doesn't really matter if we went to a great school, are on a prestigious career track, have spectacular achievements, or have raised accomplished children. What matters is that we know that God loves us and cares about who we are becoming far more than what we do or don't do.

When we can identify our eulogy virtues—the things we would want people to say about us after we die—we can identify what we value most and the person that we deeply long to become. Becoming the person we are called to be is the central drama of our lives, and yet our ongoing formation does not come as a result of our sweat and effort but as a gift of grace. The spiritual exercises we've considered in this book are not "works," but rather practices that help us become more aware of the abiding presence of God, who created us and forms us in love.

If you want to lead a life of true greatness, you don't need to travel to Mars or any other planet. You can achieve that right now, where you are, without going anywhere, as you live out the days that have been given to you for the praise of God alone. As a redeemed Whole Adam living solely for the applause of God—through the grace of Jesus Christ and by the power of the Holy Spirit—you will be set free and filled with light, joy, and contentment as you bless those around you with the gift of yourself by becoming the beautiful, beloved person God created you to be.

Questions *for* Reflection
and Discussion

———————◇———————

1. Is there an area in your life for which you long to be recognized? What is it, and why?
2. How is Jesus' definition of greatness different from the world's?
3. If most people agree that eulogy virtues are more important than resumé virtues, why do people spend so much time and energy on their resumé virtues?
4. Can you think of an example of an ordinary person who embodied true greatness?
5. How can imagining our death focus our perspective on what matters most?
6. How can you pursue everyday greatness right where you are?

THE YOKE OF GOD'S LOVE

I began this book with the story of being invited to my high school reunion. When the appointed day arrived, I put on a favorite shirt and headed out to the reunion dinner. I felt anxious as I walked toward the hotel ballroom, but there were two warm and welcoming women from my class at the reception table who put me at ease.

Over the course of the night, I found myself enjoying conservations with former classmates, most of whom I hadn't seen in years. I wasn't as prone to making comparisons as I had anticipated, and I was genuinely present to people's stories. Later that night, I reflected with Sakiko that I felt less self-conscious and far more at home with myself than I had felt during my insecure, awkward high school years.

None of us wants to go through an evening—let alone our entire lives—feeling as if we need to posture ourselves and present a persona of someone we're not in order to be accepted. We want to show up to our lives as who we really are. Whole. Confident. Satisfied in our identity as the beloved.

Thankfully, this is also what God wants for us.

Jesus says, "Come to me, all you who are weary and burdened, and I will give you rest" (Matthew 11:28). When Jesus first spoke those words, many of the people in his first-century world were anxious about whether they would have enough food for the next day, living as they were in an agrarian subsistence economy. Or, they may have been worried about their children's health, because most newborns of that time didn't live to see the age of twenty.

In our modern era, we also have concerns about finances or health matters. But we also feel angst about whether we are achieving enough, or if we are good enough—anxieties that those living during the first century would not have felt as keenly. Regardless of what wearies or burdens us, Jesus says, "Take *my* yoke upon you and learn from me . . . , and you will find rest for your souls" (Matthew 11:29, my emphasis).

When Jesus uses the word "yoke," he's describing a wooden bar placed across the back of an ox, making it easier to pull a plough or heavy load. It hardly sounds restful, does it? We'd prefer a hammock or a massage, or an all-expense paid vacation in the Caribbean. Yet what if the yoke that Jesus invites us to carry doesn't make us feel heavier but lighter? Before Jesus speaks about this yoke, he gives thanks for his relationship with his Father and rejoices that his Father in heaven knows, loves, and trusts him (Matthew 11:25). The yoke that Jesus wants to place on us is *his* yoke—the yoke that has been placed upon his shoulders by his Father in heaven—it is the yoke of his Father's love. When we wear this yoke of God's love, the burdens of our life feel lighter. This is why Jesus says, "My yoke is easy and my burden is light." When we sense God's love upon our shoulders, we are able to show up in the world with more of our whole selves. We are able to live out of the best part of our Striving Adam selves because we are not afraid to pursue actions that involve risk and possible failure. We also live out of the best part of our Soulful Adam selves as we seek to deepen our relationship with God and the people around us.

The Chilean poet Pablo Neruda wrote to his wife, "I want to do with you what spring does with the cherry trees."[1] When we are deeply loved by someone significant in our lives, we blossom into our best selves. One of the clearest analogs of this dynamic in my own life has been the relationship I've had with my mentor, Leighton Ford, whose story I first shared with you in chapter two. When I first got to know Leighton, I was in my mid-twenties, studying at a theological seminary in Boston. During that time, I was enrolled simultaneously in the pilot program of the Arrow Leadership Program, which helps develop younger emerging Christian leaders. As one of my Arrow classmates recalls, the first time our group of twenty-five or so came together, we looked sideways at one another like the fighter pilots in the movie *Top Gun*, wondering how we would fare in comparison to our rivals.

I was one of the youngest people in the class and the least experienced and accomplished in Christian ministry. At first, I was anxious to impress the founder of Arrow, Leighton Ford. I didn't want him to feel that my admission to the program had been a mistake or that his investment in me was a waste.

But during our second or third Arrow residential seminar, in the course of a conversation, Leighton looked at me with his piercing blue eyes and said, "I admire you." It felt very special. With the passing of years, I got a deeper sense that his love and care for me were independent of any benefit that I could offer him, or his organization, or even to the larger world of Christian ministry. I found his commitment to me has been unwavering in the midst of all my limitations, vulnerabilities, and failures. Now, twenty-five years later, I feel more loved and at home in his presence than ever. I feel free to be transparent about my struggles and temptations as well as to share without inhibition the joys of my life.

It's not that I no longer want to make something of my life and ministry, in part to honor his generous love for and investment in me. But now that desire comes out of a place of gratitude and love rather than fear or the desperate hunger to be validated.

This is also true in my relationship with God. Thanks largely to the practices that I have outlined in this book—such as silent prayer, Sabbath keeping, and serving—I've become much more aware of God's love for me, which has always been present in my life. I feel far less anxious about needing to do something to earn God's approval because I know I am a beloved son. Yet I also want to do my best for God out of a deep sense of love, reverence, and gratitude.

This is my hope and prayer for you as well.

May you live more and more fully into the knowledge that the Creator of the universe cherishes you as a son or daughter.

May the practices touched on in this book deepen your awareness that you are a beloved child of grace.

May you become fully present, confident, and engaged in your life as you take on the yoke of God's love and lay down the exhausting burden of living as an insecure facsimile of yourself.

May you live a life of daring courageousness, depth, and relationship as you come to be loved and to love more and more fully and more and more abundantly.

ACKNOWLEDGMENTS

In the chapter on gratitude, I write that each step of our journey traces a story of grace. This has certainly been true of this book. While I take ownership of all its shortcomings, I could not have pursued this project without the grace of God and the generosity of many people.

Thank you, Leighton Ford, for stimulating the idea for this book by sharing the link to David Brooks' talk on the inverse logic of life.

Karen Hollenbeck, your wisdom and mastery with words helped bring order from chaos.

Mark Buchanan, I am grateful for your friendship and your generous, sage counsel on the writing process.

Julia Cheung, thank you for lending me your sensibility for language and your candor.

Peter Mitham, I am grateful for your capacity to help me express myself with more clarity.

Thank you to the board of elders and the Tenth community for enabling the rhythms that allow me to write.

To our Tenth Church site pastors Jade Holownia, Andrew Cheung, Dan Matheson, and Jay Ewing, and also to Penny Crosby, who offer substantive and straightforward input on my (and our) speaking and writing: I am thankful for the growth you foster in my ministry and life.

I am grateful to Jason Byassee, Sarah Tsang, Erin Gagner, Sabine Lague, Andy Crouch, Curtis Chang, Mi-Jung Lee, Winnie Su, Susan Phillips, Joanna Mockler, Parker Palmer, Milissa Ewing, Craig Pagens, Kristin Werner, Elizabeth Archer-Klein, Zack Eswine, Eric Taylor, Chris Woodhull, James Petersen, Omar Hamada, Sam Rima, Allison Barfoot, Joshua Dunford, Joshua Harris, Nick Valadez, Rob Des Cotes, Marian de Gier, Brian Liu, Claudia McKenzie, Paul Yokota, Yasushi Tomono, Carol Wallace, James Bryan Smith, Dan Brunner, Scott Gibson, John Ortberg, Gordon T. Smith, and Darrell Johnson for your friendship and responding to early drafts of the book or stimulating ideas for it.

Thank you, Ann Voskamp, for writing the foreword and making me feel like I was doing you the favor!

Thank you Glenn Lucke, Timothy McConnell, and Zach Spilman of the Docent Research Group.

To Ryan Pazdur, Nathan Kroeze, Greg Clouse, Paul Pastor, Stephanie Anderson, Trinity McFadden, and the team at Zondervan, thank you for believing in this project and for all you have invested in it. It is a pleasure and privilege to work with you!

To Edlyn Hiebert, I am grateful for all you do to make my ministry (and life) work!

I'm also thankful for my siblings: Rie, Setsu, Hana, and Tetsuro for your love and candid feedback.

Thank you, Ken Nixon, for your faithful friendship and amazingly generous support.

Thank you, Mom and Dad, for living the message of this

book before I wrote a word of it. (While I was writing the book, my dad passed from this life to the next. I look forward to expressing more gratitude to him in the world to come.)

Thank you to my wife Sakiko—what a joy to share the journey of life, love, and writing with you! Joey, your existence reminds us of God's great love.

And thank you to the triune God: Father, Son, and Holy Spirit, for your generosity far beyond what I deserve. To you alone be the glory.

NOTES

Introduction

1. Alain De Botton, "A Kinder, Gentler Philosophy of Success," *TED Talk | TED.com*, July 2009. See also Alain De Botton, *Status Anxiety* (Toronto: Penguin Group Canada, 2005).

Chapter 1: The Divided Self

1. Quoted from the Berean Bible Translation.
2. Joseph B. Soloveitchik, *The Lonely Man of Faith* (New York: Doubleday, 2006), 9–19.
3. Ibid., 20–26.
4. I am paraphrasing Edwin H. Friedman, Margaret M. Treadwell, and Edward W. Beal, *A Failure of Nerve: Leadership in the Age of the Quick Fix* (New York: Seabury Books, 2007), 8.
5. Walter Isaacson, *Steve Jobs* (New York: Simon and Schuster, 2011), 104.
6. Shawn Achor, *The Happiness Advantage: The Seven Principles That Fuel Success and Performance at Work* (London: Virgin, 2011), 3.
7. Psychologist Shawn Achor notes that when our brains are in a positive, happy mode, they are 31 percent more productive than in a negative or stressed mode. Salespeople perform 37 percent better, and doctors are 19 percent faster and more accurate with diagnoses when in a positive mindset versus a neutral or a negative one. Shawn Achor, "The Happy Secret to Better Work," *TED Talk | TED.com*, May 2011, https://www.ted.com/

talks/shawn_achor_the_happy_secret_to_better_work. Achor
develops the idea in his book *The Happiness Advantage*.

Chapter 2: The Whole Self

1. Henri J. M. Nouwen, *Life of the Beloved: Spiritual Living in a Secular World* (New York: Crossroad, 1992), 31.
2. St. Augustine, *Confessions*, 6.6 (Oxford: Oxford University Press, 2008), 9.
3. Peter Brown, *Augustine of Hippo: A Biography* (Berkeley: Univ. of California Press, 1984), 32.
4. David Brooks, *The Road to Character* (New York: Random House, 2015), 192.
5. Augustine, *Confessions*, 1.1, 3.
6. Ibid., 6.6, 108.
7. Ibid., 8.7, 145.
8. St. Augustine, *Confessions*, 6.6 (Harmondsworth: Penguin, 1961), 104.
9. Brown, *Augustine of Hippo*, 131.
10. Richard Foster, *Streams of Living Water: Essential Practices from the Six Great Traditions of Christian Faith* (New York: Harper, 1998), 193.
11. Philip F. Reinders, *Seeking God's Face: Praying with the Bible through the Year* (Grand Rapids: Baker, 2010), 399.

Chapter 3: Spiritual Practices

1. Richard J. Foster, *Celebration of Discipline: The Path to Spiritual Growth*, 1st ed. (San Francisco: Harper and Row, 1978), 6.
2. Henri J. M Nouwen, *Life of the Beloved*, 30–31.
3. Timothy Noxon, "Myers-Briggs Type Indicator (MBT1) and Christian Spirituality," accessed January 20, 2017, http://thenoxfactor.com/files/NoxonMyers-Briggs.pdf.

Chapter 4: Meditation

1. Peter Scazzero, *Daily Office: Remembering God's Presence Throughout the Day* (Elmhurst, N.Y.: Willow Creek Press, 2008), 4.

2. Cited in Thomas Keating, *Intimacy with God: An Introduction to Centering Prayer* (New York: Crossroad, 2009), 38.

3. Gerald G. May, *Addiction and Grace*, Leader's Guide (San Francisco: Harper SanFrancisco, 1991), 3–9.

4. M. S. Laird, *Into the Silent Land: A Guide to the Christian Practice of Contemplation* (Oxford: Oxford University Press, 2006), 20–22.

5. Keating, *Intimacy with God*, 16.

6. Ibid., 73.

7. Kelly McGonigal, *The Willpower Instinct: How Self-Control Works, Why It Matters, and What You Can Do to Get More of It* (New York: Avery, 2012), 27–28.

8. Ibid., 24–29.

9. Palmer, *Let Your Life Speak*, 30.

10. Keating, *Intimacy with God*, 51–55.

11. Laird, *Into the Silent Land*, 3, 29.

Chapter 5: Sabbath

1. Walter Brueggemann, *Sabbath as Resistance: Saying No to the Culture of Now* (Louisville: Westminster John Knox Press, 2014), xiii–xiv.

2. This observation is made by Pico Iyer, "The Art of Stillness," n.d., https://www.ted.com/talks/pico_iyer_the_art_of_stillness/ transcript.

3. Peter Scazzero, *The Emotionally Healthy Leader: How Transforming Your Inner Life Will Deeply Transform Your Church, Team, and the World* (Grand Rapids: Zondervan, 2015), 159–60.

4. Thomas Cahill and the Mazal Holocaust Collection, *The Gifts of the Jews: How a Tribe of Desert Nomads Changed the Way Everyone Thinks and Feels* (New York: Nan A. Talese, 1998), 144.

5. I am paraphrasing Chris Wiman, n.d., https://imagejournal.org/ article/gods-truth-life/.

6. Daniel J. Levitin, *The Organized Mind: Thinking Straight in the Age of Information Overload* (New York, N.Y.: Dutton, 2014), 185.

7. Eugene H. Peterson, *Working the Angles: The Shape of Pastoral*

Integrity (Grand Rapids: Eerdmans, 1987), 62–83. I am also drawing from Psalm 92.

8. Mark Buchanan, *The Rest of God: Restoring Your Soul by Restoring Sabbath* (Nashville: Thomas Nelson, 2006), 126.

9. Cited in Eugene H. Peterson, *The Contemplative Pastor: Returning to the Art of Spiritual Direction*, vol. 17 of *The Leadership Library* (Carol Stream, Ill.: Word, 1989), 28.

10. McGonigal, *The Willpower Instinct*, 137.

11. Levitin, *The Organized Mind*, 101–2.

12. R. Paul Stevens and Alvin Ung, *Taking Your Soul to Work: Overcoming the Nine Deadly Sins of the Workplace* (Grand Rapids: Eerdmans, 2010), 155.

13. Eugene Peterson, The Message, Matthew 11:28–30.

14. Reinders, *Seeking God's Face*, 183.

Chapter 6: Gratitude

1. David Steindl-Rast, "Want to Be Happy? Be Grateful," *TED Talk | TED.com*, June 2013, https://www.ted.com/talks/david_steindl _rast_want_to_be_happy_be_grateful#t-60096.

2. See Robert Emmons and M. E. McCullough, *Journal of Psychology* (2003): 84, 377–389.

3. Matthieu Ricard, "The Habits of Happiness," *TED Talk | TED.com*, February 2004, https://www.ted.com/talks/matthieu_ricard_on _the_habits_of_happiness.

4. Ann Voskamp, *One Thousand Gifts: A Dare to Live Fully Right Where You Are* (Grand Rapids: Zondervan, 2010).

5. Achor, *The Happiness Advantage*, 100–101.

6. Mason Currey, *Daily Rituals: How Artists Work* (New York: Alfred A. Knopf, 2013).

7. Ibid., 9.

8. Cited in Anne Lamott, *Bird by Bird: Some Instructions on Writing and Life* (New York: Anchor Books, 1995), 6–10.

9. I am adapting an idea from John Ortberg, *Soul Keeping: Caring for the Most Important Part of You* (Grand Rapids: Zondervan, 2014), 169.

10. Ibid., 172.
11. I learned about Colman's character in part through my conversations with his wife Joanna Mockler.
12. John Ortberg, *Soul Keeping*, 22–30, 61.

Chapter 7: Simple Abundance

1. Richard J. Foster, *Freedom of Simplicity: Finding Harmony in a Complex World* (San Francisco: HarperSanFrancisco, 2005), 9.
2. James Bryan Smith, *The Good and Beautiful Life: Putting on the Character of Christ* (Downers Grove, Ill.: InterVarsity Press, 2009), 163–64.
3. Malcolm Gladwell, *David and Goliath: Underdogs, Misfits, and the Art of Battling Giants* (New York: Little, Brown and Company, 2013), 49.
4. Rakesh Kochhar, "A Global Middle Class Is More Promise than Reality: From 2001 to 2011. Nearly 7 Million Step Out of Poverty, but Most Only Barely" (Washington, D.C.: Pew Research Center, July 2015).
5. I write about these rhythms in Ken Shigematsu, *God in My Everything: How an Ancient Rhythm Helps Busy People Enjoy God* (Grand Rapids: Zondervan, 2013). See also Dallas Willard, cited in *Soul Keeping*, 89.
6. Michael Yankoski, *The Sacred Year: Mapping the Soulscape of Spiritual Practice—How Contemplating Apples, Living in a Cave, and Befriending a Dying Woman Revived My Life* (Nashville: Thomas Nelson, 2014), 76.
7. Ibid., 77.
8. Daniel Gilbert, "The Surprising Science of Happiness," *TED Talk | TED.com*, February 2004, https://www.ted.com/talks/dan_gilbert_asks_why_are_we_happy.
9. Nicholas D. Kristof and Sheryl WuDunn, *Half the Sky: Turning Oppression into Opportunity for Women Worldwide* (New York: Vintage, 2010), 250.
10. Reinders, *Seeking God's Face*, 757.

Chapter 8: Servanthood

1. The idea for this illustration was inspired in a sermon by Tim Ghali, "Loyalty Tests and Dirty Feet," February 22, 2015, http://www.grace.org/sermon/loyalty-tests-and-dirty-feet/.
2. Andy Crouch, *Playing God: Redeeming the Gift of Power* (Downers Grove, Ill.: InterVarsity Press, 2013), 161–66.
3. Foster, *Celebration of Discipline*, 113–14.
4. Dorothy Day, *The Long Loneliness: The Autobiography of Dorothy Day* (San Francisco: Harper and Row, 1981).
5. Brooks, *The Road to Character*, 92.
6. Crouch, *Playing God*, 242.

Chapter 9: Friendship

1. Gregory of Nazianzus, *Select Orations*, trans. Martha Pollard Vinson, vol. 107 of *The Fathers of the Church* (Washington, D.C.: Catholic University of America Press, 2003), 30.
2. McGonigal, *The Willpower Instinct*, 188.
3. Liz Carmichael, *Friendship: Interpreting Christian Love* (London: T & T Clark, 2004).
4. Augustine, 2.5 *Confessions*, 29.
5. René Girard, *Deceit, Desire, and the Novel: Self and Other in Literary Structure*, trans. Yvonne Freccero (Baltimore: Johns Hopkins University Press, 1998), 12.
6. McGonigal, *The Willpower Instinct*, 194–95.
7. Brooks, *The Road to Character*, 7.
8. I am drawing this data from Robert Waldinger, "What Makes a Good Life? Lessons from the Longest Study on Happiness," *TED Talk | TED.com*, (November 2015), https://www.ted.com/talks/robert_waldinger_what_makes_a_good_life_lessons_from_the_longest_study_on_happiness.
9. Aristotle and Terence Irwin, *Nicomachean Ethics*, 2nd ed. (Indianapolis: Hackett, 1999), 122.
10. C. S. Lewis, *The Four Loves* (New York: Harcourt Brace Jovanovich, 1960), 89.

11. Carmichael, *Friendship*, 16.
12. My reflections in this chapter on prioritizing family and friendship are largely informed and inspired by Clayton M. Christensen, James Allworth, and Karen Dillon, *How Will You Measure Your Life?* (New York: Harper Business, 2012), 75.
13. Hugh Black, "Friendship," n.d., http://www.hotfreebooks.com/book/Friendship-Hugh-Black.html.
14. C. Stephen Jaeger, "Alcuin and the Music of Friendship," *MLN* 127, no. 6 (2012): 105–25.
15. The spiritual direction movement is growing, and there are now more than six thousand spiritual directors under the banner of Spiritual Directors International, most of whom serve in North America.
16. Gordon T. Smith, *Spiritual Direction: A Guide to Giving and Receiving Direction* (Downers Grove, Ill.: InterVarsity Press, 2014), 10.
17. Susan S. Phillips, *Candlelight: Illuminating the Art of Spiritual Direction* (Harrisburg, Pa.: Morehouse, 2008).
18. Hebrews 10:24–25, NLT.
19. "Faithandworship.com," n.d., http://www.faithandworship.com/Celtic Blessings and Prayers.htm.

Chapter 10: Vocation

1. Palmer, *Let Your Life Speak*, 4.
2. Leo Tolstoy, *The Death of Ivan Ilyich and Other Stories* (London: Penguin, 2008), 210.
3. Ibid., 216.
4. James Martin, *The Jesuit Guide to (Almost) Everything: A Spirituality for Real Life* (New York: HarperCollins, 2010), 207–8.
5. Chris Lowney, *Heroic Leadership: Best Practices from a 450-Year-Old Company That Changed the World* (Chicago: Loyola Press, 2005), 121.
6. Andy Crouch, *Strong and Weak: Embracing a Life of Love, Risk and True Flourishing* (2016), 23.
7. C. S. Lewis, *Letters to Malcolm: Chiefly on Prayer* (New York: Harcourt, Brace and World, 1964), 92–93.

8. For further reflection on the examen and discernment, see Thomas H. Green, *Weeds Among the Wheat: Discernment, Where Prayer and Action Meet* (Notre Dame, Ind.: Ave Maria Press, 1984).

Chapter 11: Redefining Greatness

1. Brooks, *The Road to Character*, 7.
2. C. S. Lewis, *The Great Divorce: A Dream* (San Francisco: HarperSanFrancisco, 2001), 118–20.
3. George Eliot, *Middlemarch* (1872; reprint, New York: Modern Library Classics, 2000), preface, 2.
4. Ibid., 799.

Epilogue

1. Pablo Neruda, *Twenty Love Poems and a Song of Despair*, trans. W. S. Merwin (1969; reprint, San Francisco: Chronicle Books, 1993), 55.